A B C D E F G H I J K L M

THE ILLUSTRATED
ENCYCLOPEDIA

VOLUME 8

T-Z

Belitha Press

N O P Q R S T U V W X Y Z

First published 1995 by
Macmillan Education Australia Pty Ltd

First published in the United Kingdom in 1995 by
Belitha Press Limited
31 Newington Green, London N16 9PU

Cataloguing in print data available from the British Library.

ISBN 1 85561 527 4 (Vol 8)
ISBN 1 85561 529 0 (Set)

Consultant: Frances Warhurst
UK editor: Maria O'Neill
Project editor: Jo Higgins

Typeset by Polar Design
Printed in Hong Kong

Acknowledgements

The author and publishers are grateful to the following for permission to reproduce copyright photographs:

Cover: Northside Photographics

Air France, p. 19 (centre); Australia Picture Library, p. 43 (top); Bruce Coleman, p. 43 (bottom left); Coo-ee Picture Library, pp. 9 (top right), 12, 13, 14, 15 (bottom left & right), 17 (top), 19 (left), 21 (left top & bottom), 24 (top & centre right), 27 (top), 26, 27, 29, 37 (top), 39 (right), 40 (right), 44, 46 (left), 46 & 47, 50 (left), 52 (left), 57, 58, 60, 64 (bottom & top right); CSIRO Australia Telescope, pp. 8 & 9; Nigel Dennis/A.N.T. Photo Library, pp. 34 (bottom left & right), 63 (centre top); Carole Elchert, p. 61 (bottom); Marten Harvey/A.N.T. Photo Library, pp. 5 (right), 55 (bottom right); John Higgins, pp. 21 (bottom right), 38; Gerard Lacz/A.N.T. Photo Library, 35 (top), 55 (top), 64 (bottom left); Lego, pp. 15 (top left), 50 & 51; Dale Mann/ Retrospect, p. 17 (bottom); NASA, pp. 11 (bottom), 18 (bottom right); NHPA/A.N.T. Photo Library, pp. 42 & 43, 54, 55; Northern Territory Tourist Commission, p. 38 (left); Northside Photographics, pp. 4 (bottom), 5 (bottom left), 9 (top left), 11 (top), 24 (bottom right), 27 (top left), 31 (top left), 37 (bottom) © Robert Moore, 51 (centre), 53 (bottom right), 59, 61 (top), 62 & 63, 63 (centre bottom) © Brian Carroll; Chase Parker/A.N.T. Photo Library, p. 25 (left); Silvestris/A.N.T. Photo Library, p. 63 (top); Sporting Pix, p. 41 (top & bottom left); Telecom Australia, p. 7 (top and bottom); Dave Watts/A.N.T. Photo Library, p. 49 (top); Wild Nature/A.N.T. Photo Library, p. 31 (top right & bottom).

While every care has been taken to trace and acknowledge copyright the publishers tender their apologies for any accidental infringement where copyright has proved untraceable.

Illustrators
Sharyn Madder: 20, 21, 38, 42, 43, 54, 55, 61, 62, 63
Rhyll Plant: 13, 28, 29, 32, 33, 36, 37, 44, 47, 52, 53, 56, 57
John Fairbridge: 14, 15, 16, 17, 18, 19, 22, 23, 50, 51, 58
Paul Konye: 6, 7, 8, 12, 40, 41, 59, 60
Andrew Plant: 24, 25, 26, 30, 34, 35, 48, 49
Xiangyi Mo: 4, 5, 10, 11

HOW TO USE THIS BOOK

The Illustrated Encyclopedia has over 300 entries. The entries are arranged alphabetically. To find your topic, use the guide letters at the top of each page to check you have the right volume. The first letter of your topic will be highlighted.

TOPIC: TELEPHONE

guide letter

N O P Q R S **T** U V W X Y Z

Use the guide words printed in the top right-hand corner of each page to find your topic. The guide words list the entries on a double-page spread. They are listed alphabetically. Check the guide words to see if you need to go backwards or forwards.

guide word

TELEPHONE

You can also use the index in Volume 9 to find your topic.

telephone
Volume 4 60
Volume 7 35
Volume 8 **6–7**

If you cannot find your topic in its alphabetical order in the encyclopedia, use the index.

tadpole
see amphibian
see frog
see life cycle

TOPIC: TADPOLE

The index lists all the topics in alphabetical order. It tells you where you will find your topic.

More information on how to use the encyclopedia and the index can be found in Volume 9.

TASTE

SEE ALSO • Brain • Ears • Eye • Human Body • Nose • Skin

Taste is one of the senses that animals and people use when they are eating. We can taste food because we have taste buds on our tongue.

TASTE BUDS

Taste buds are found on your tongue. Taste buds tell your brain whether something is salty, sour, bitter or sweet.

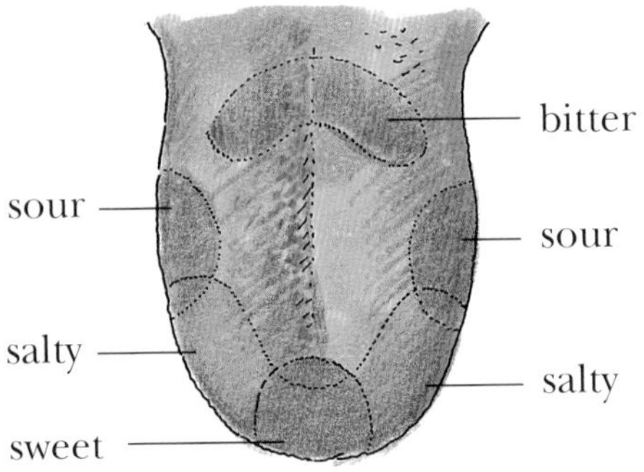

SENSE OF SMELL ▼

For many animals, such as these quolls, the sense of smell is the most important sense. They use it to find food and mates, and to detect danger.

TASTE AND SMELL

Taste and smell work together. When you have a cold and lose your sense of smell, food does not taste the same.

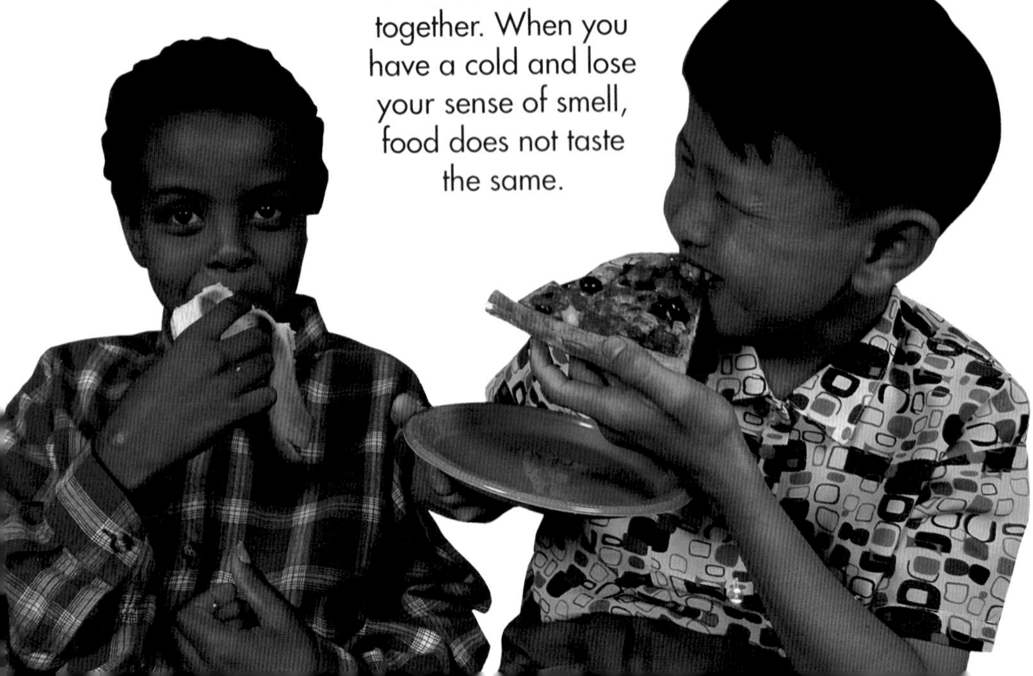

THE FIVE SENSES

Humans have five senses. These are touch, hearing, taste, smell and sight.

INTERESTING FACT

Flies have taste receptors on their feet. They taste food when they land on it.

TEETH

SEE ALSO • Digestion • Human Body • Rodents

Teeth are hard, white and bony and grow in your mouth. They grow on the upper and lower jaws. Teeth are used to cut, bite and chew food.

PARTS OF A TOOTH

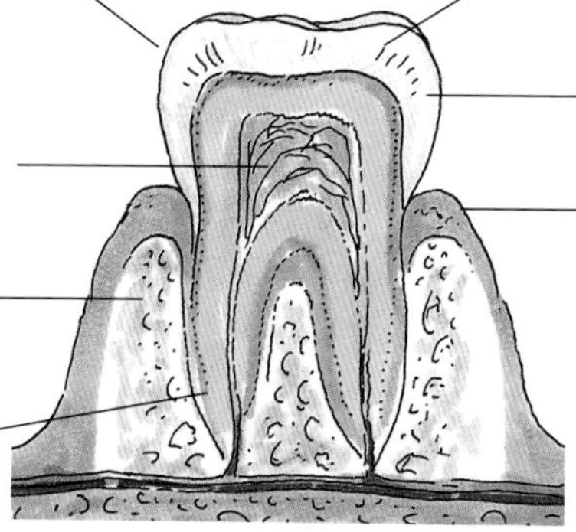

PLAQUE

Bacteria form a coating of plaque on your teeth. Brushing your teeth removes plaque and keeps your teeth and gums healthy.

TEETH AS WEAPONS

Many animals such as cheetahs use their teeth as weapons to kill prey.

INTERESTING FACT

Enamel on teeth is the hardest part of your body.

HUMAN TEETH

Humans grow two sets of teeth – milk teeth and permanent teeth.

- Most children start to grow milk teeth before they are one year old. There are usually 20 milk teeth.
- Between the ages of 6 and 12, the milk teeth are replaced by permanent teeth.

An adult usually has 32 teeth, 16 in each jaw.

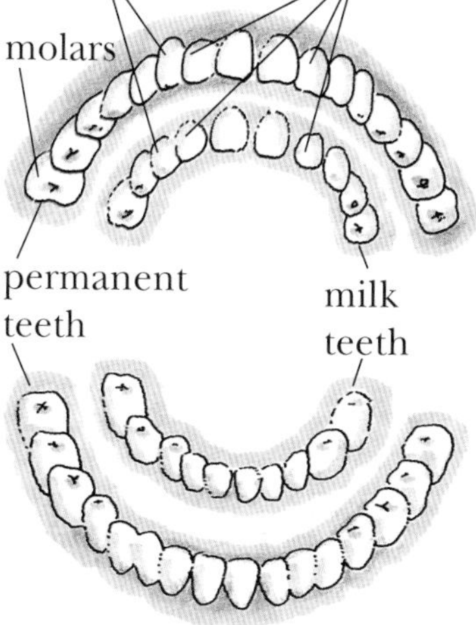

There are four main kinds of teeth: incisors, canines, molars and wisdom teeth. Wisdom teeth are the last four teeth to grow. They may not grow until people are 18 or older. Sometimes they don't grow at all.

TELEPHONE

SEE ALSO • Laser • Radar • Radio • Satellite

A telephone is a machine. You can use it to talk to someone who is close by or far away. A telephone changes the sound of your voice into electrical signals at one end and back to the sound of your voice at the other end.

PARTS OF A TELEPHONE

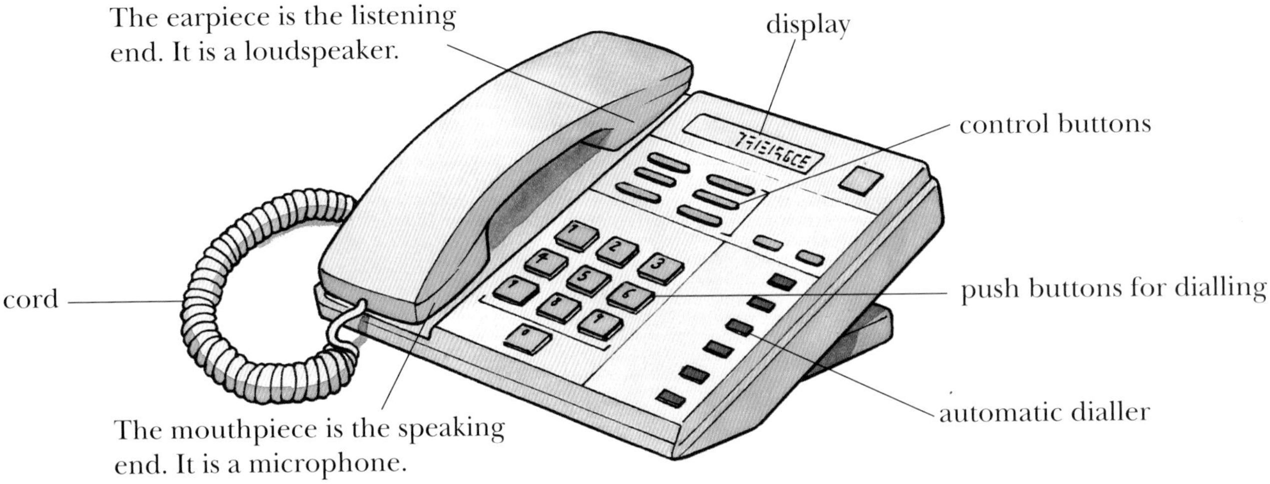

HOW A TELEPHONE WORKS

Every telephone has its own number. When you dial a number, the telephone sends electrical signals to the telephone exchange. The exchange automatically connects you to the number dialled.

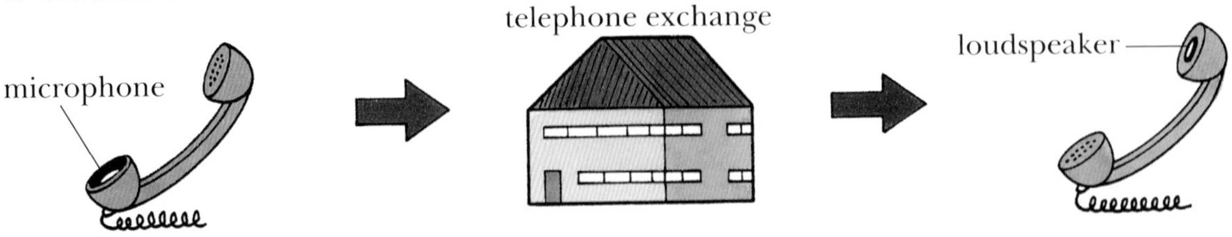

1. Inside the mouthpiece there is a microphone. The microphone changes the sound of your voice into electrical signals.

2. The electrical signals travel along wires to the earpiece of another telephone.

3. Inside the earpiece there is a loudspeaker. The loudspeaker changes the electrical signals back into the sound of your voice.

◀ A TELEPHONE EXCHANGE

Most telephone exchanges are computerized. Computers make the connections which link two telephones.

Fax machines use telephone lines to send copies of text and pictures to fax machines in other places.

HISTORY

The first telephone was invented by Alexander Graham Bell in 1876.

TELEPHONE NETWORKS

You can make a telephone call from just about anywhere in the world to anyone. Telephone calls to other countries can travel along optical fibre cables or by satellite.

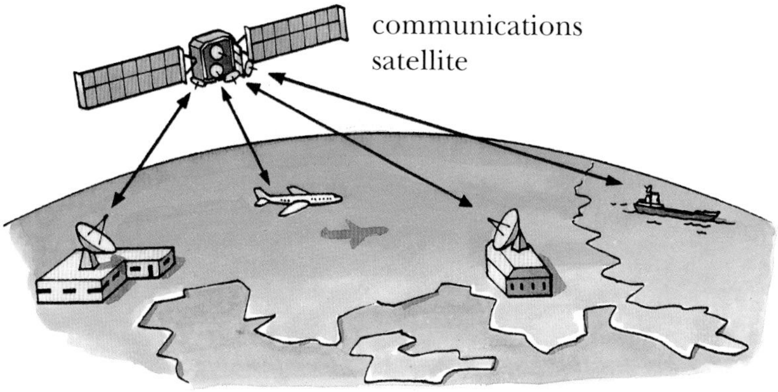

- Communications satellites receive telephone calls from one country and send them to another country.
- Optical fibre cables are made of glass. Each fibre is as fine as a human hair. Telephone conversations carried along these cables are changed into pulses of laser light. ▶

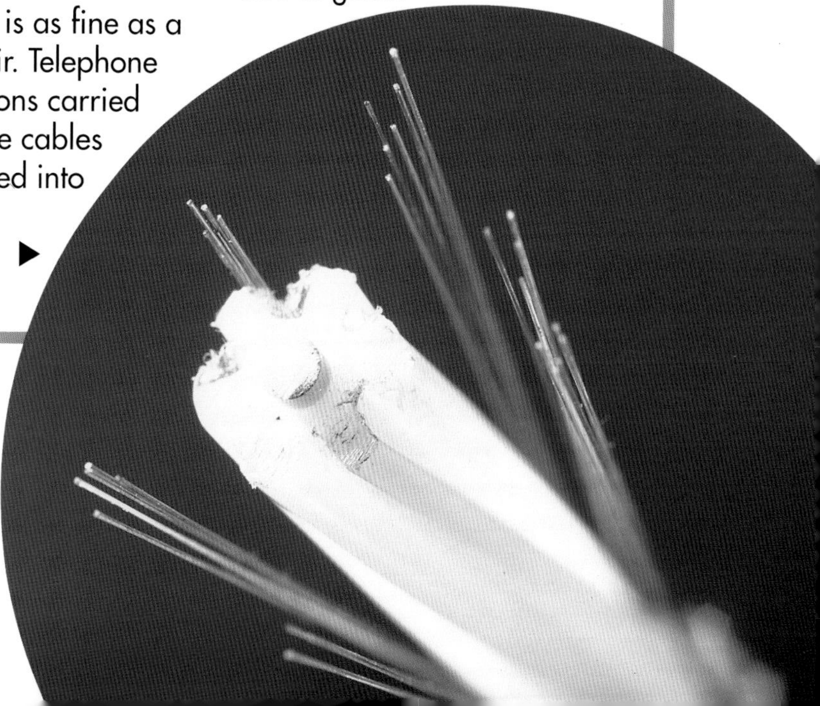

PORTABLE PHONES

A portable or mobile phone does not have a cord. It has a built-in radio transmitter and receiver.

INTERESTING FACT

The word telephone comes from two Greek words – 'tele' which means 'far' and 'phone' which means 'sound from far away'.

TELESCOPE

SEE ALSO • Astronomy • Galaxy • Meteor • Star • Universe

A telescope is an instrument. It makes objects that are far away seem closer. Telescopes also make things look bigger than they are. When the telescope was invented in the seventeenth century, people began to learn about the Universe.

KINDS OF TELESCOPES

There are two kinds of telescopes.

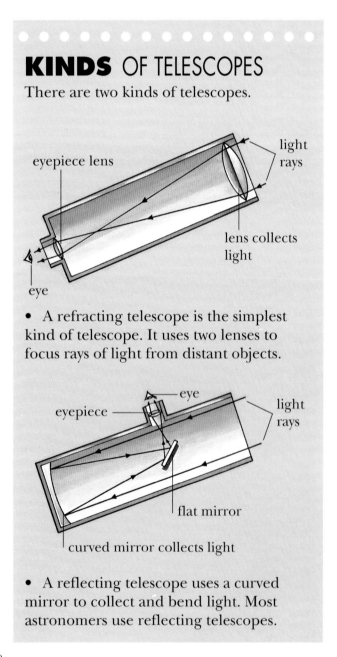

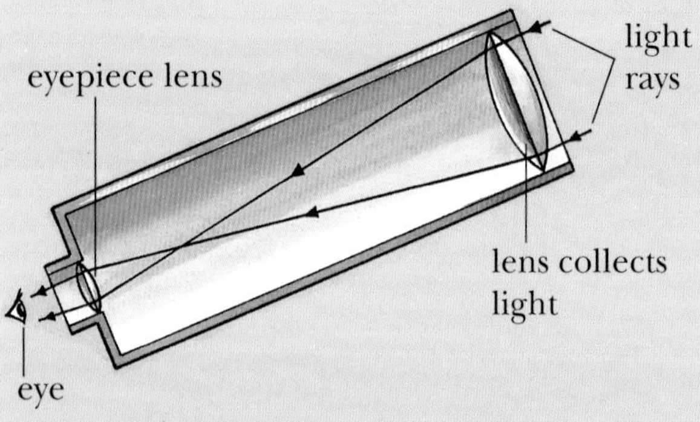

• A refracting telescope is the simplest kind of telescope. It uses two lenses to focus rays of light from distant objects.

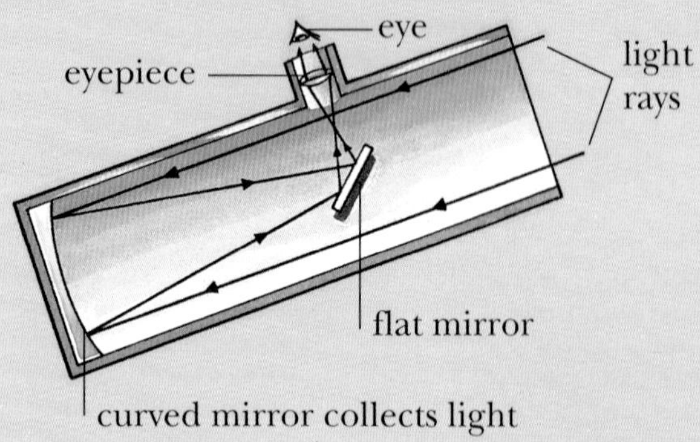

• A reflecting telescope uses a curved mirror to collect and bend light. Most astronomers use reflecting telescopes.

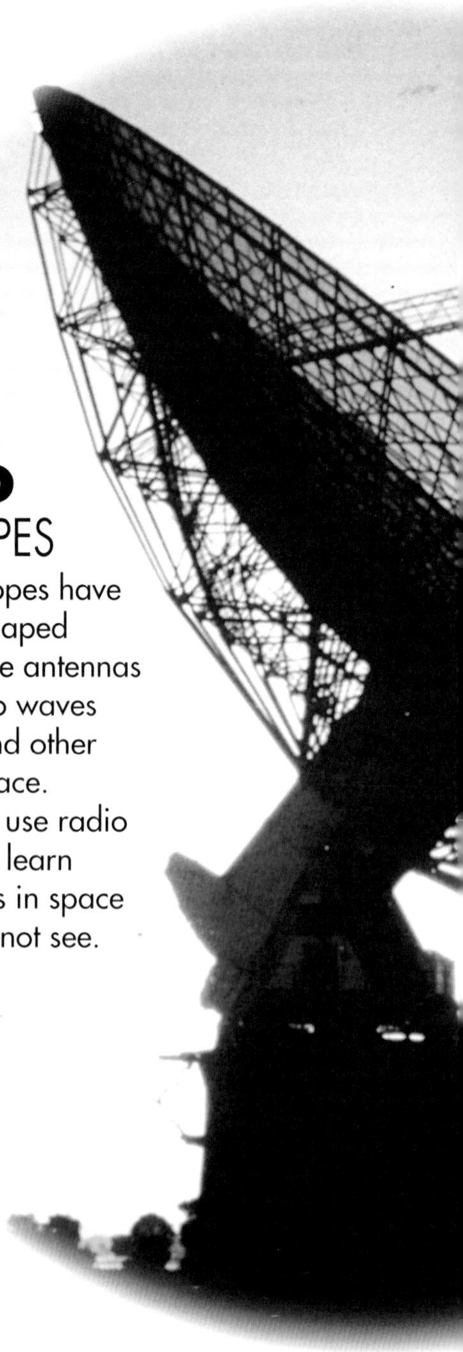

RADIO TELESCOPES

Radio telescopes have large dish-shaped antennas. The antennas pick up radio waves from stars and other objects in space. Astronomers use radio telescopes to learn about objects in space that they cannot see.

BINOCULARS

Binoculars are a kind of double telescope, one for each eye.

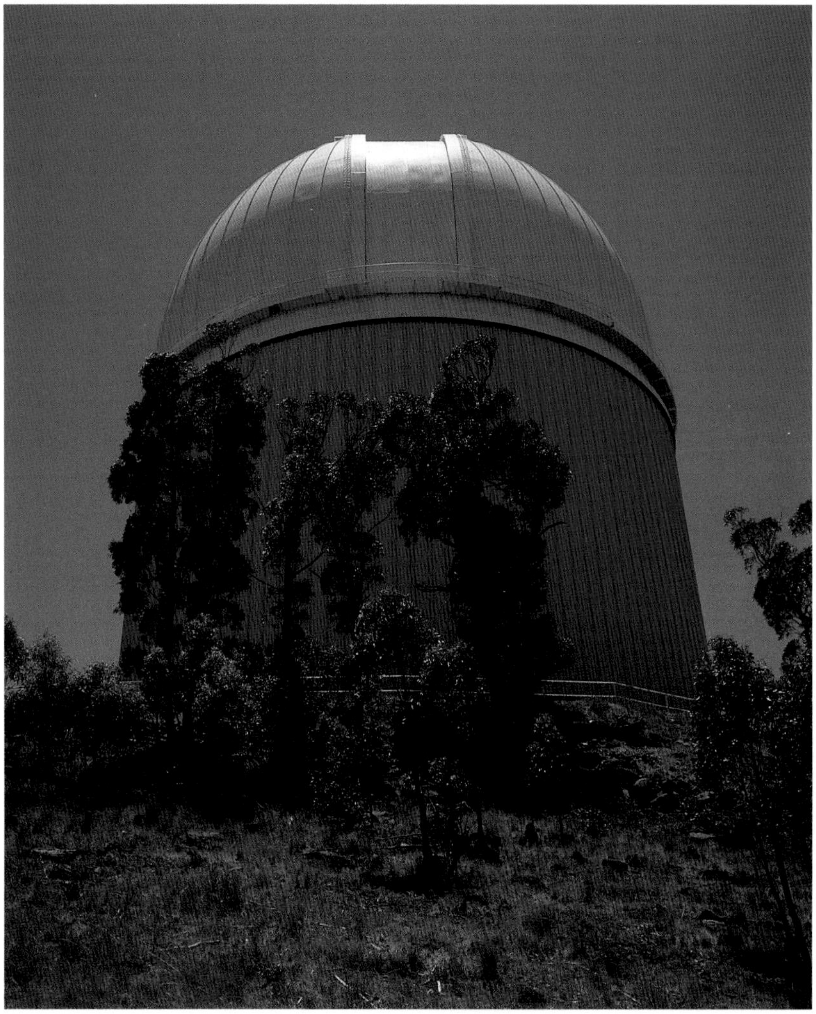

▲

AN OBSERVATORY

Astronomers work in an observatory. They use powerful modern telescopes to find out about stars, galaxies and planets.

Astronomers programme computers to direct the telescope to the right galaxy, star or planet. ▶

TELEVISION

SEE ALSO • Camera • Radio • Satellite • Telephone

Television is a way of sending sound and picture signals through the air. A television set turns the signals into sound and pictures. Television programmes are sent via cables, telephone wires and radio signals.

HOW COLOUR TELEVISION WORKS

• The pictures you see on your television are filmed by a special camera. The camera records a picture of the scene. The picture is changed into electrical signals. Colour television cameras split up a picture into red, blue and green. The microphone picks up sound which is turned into electrical signals. Electrical signals of sound and pictures are sent to a television transmitter.

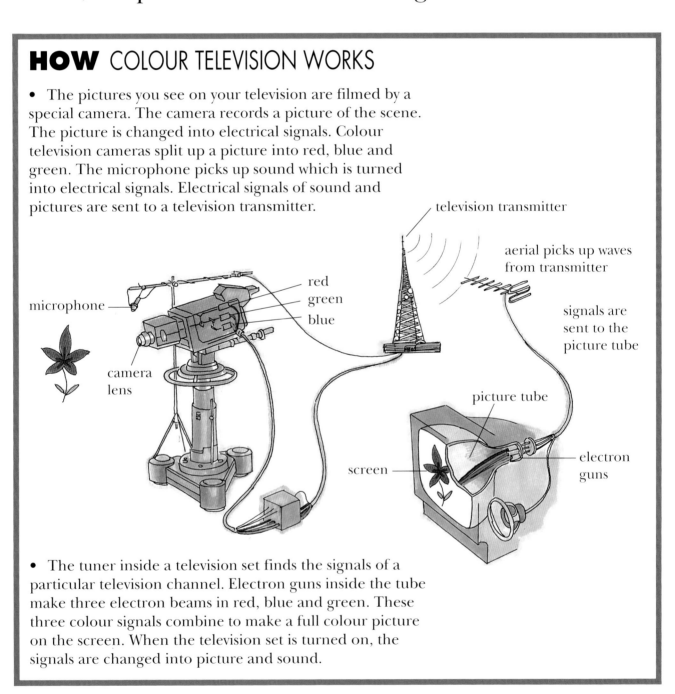

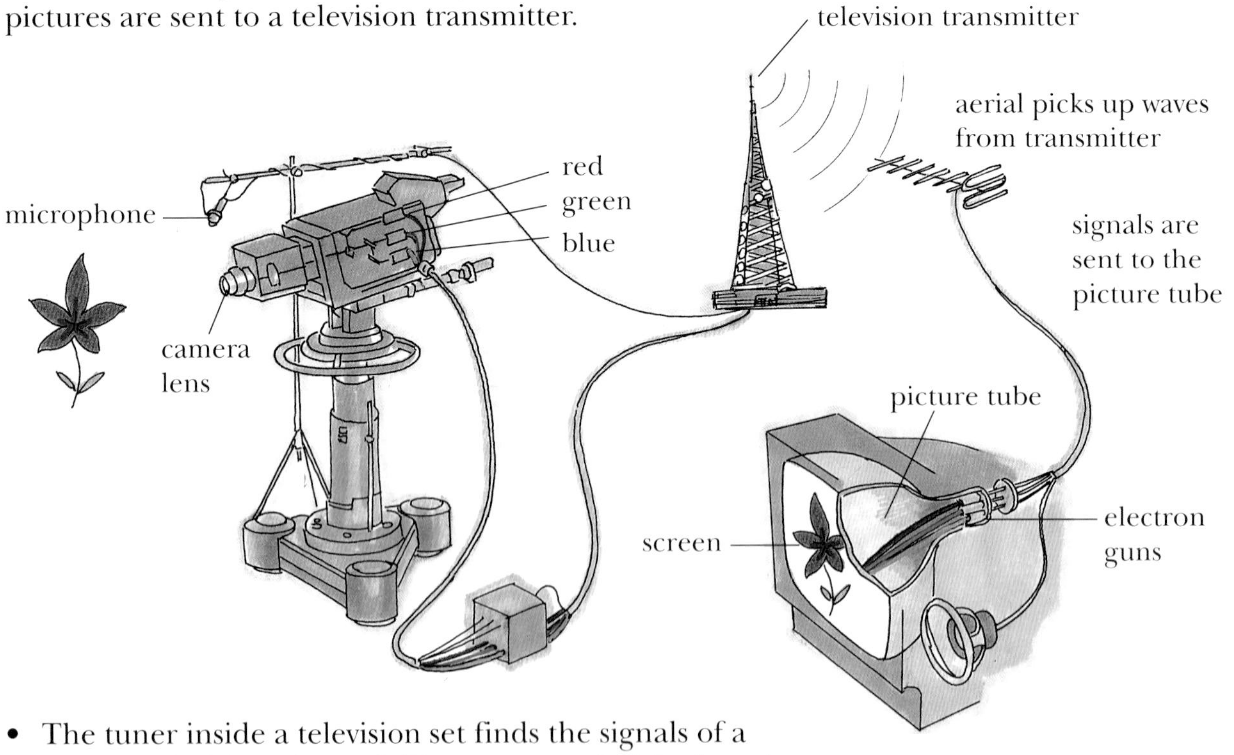

• The tuner inside a television set finds the signals of a particular television channel. Electron guns inside the tube make three electron beams in red, blue and green. These three colour signals combine to make a full colour picture on the screen. When the television set is turned on, the signals are changed into picture and sound.

INSIDE A TELEVISION STUDIO

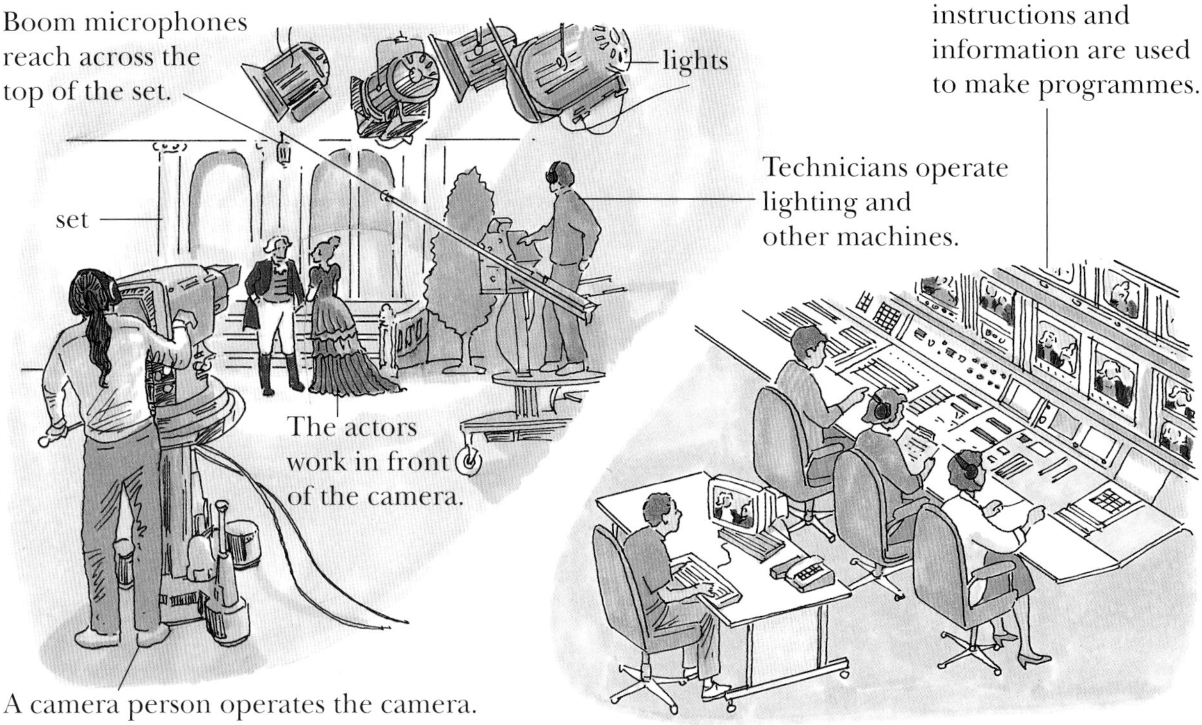
Boom microphones reach across the top of the set.
lights
Control room where instructions and information are used to make programmes.
Technicians operate lighting and other machines.
set
The actors work in front of the camera.
A camera person operates the camera.

CLOSED-CIRCUIT TELEVISION

Closed-circuit television is useful for checking on traffic. It is also used by security guards in banks and shops.

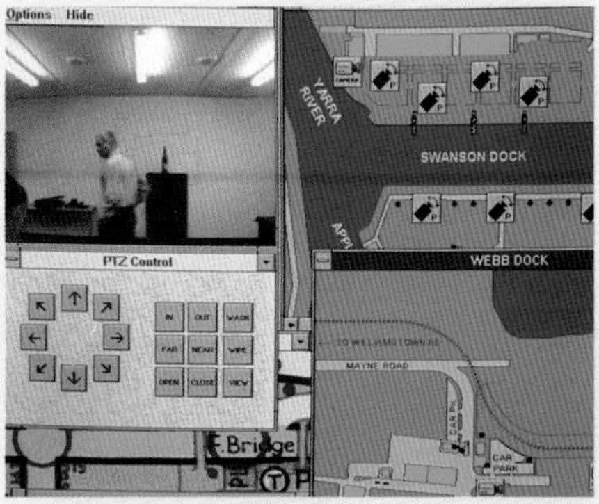
Options Hide
PTZ Control
YARRA RIVER
SWANSON DOCK
WEBB DOCK
MAYNE ROAD
F.Bridge

INTERESTING FACT

The first television show was shown in Britain in 1936. Colour television began in the USA in 1956.

VIDEOS

Video tapes store picture and sound signals on magnetic tape. The tape can be played on a video cassette recorder (VCR) which is connected to a television.

SATELLITES

Television signals can be sent around the world via satellite.

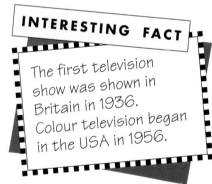

TENNIS

SEE ALSO • Cricket

Tennis is a game in which a ball is hit over a net with a racket.

A TENNIS COURT

Tennis is played on a specially marked court.

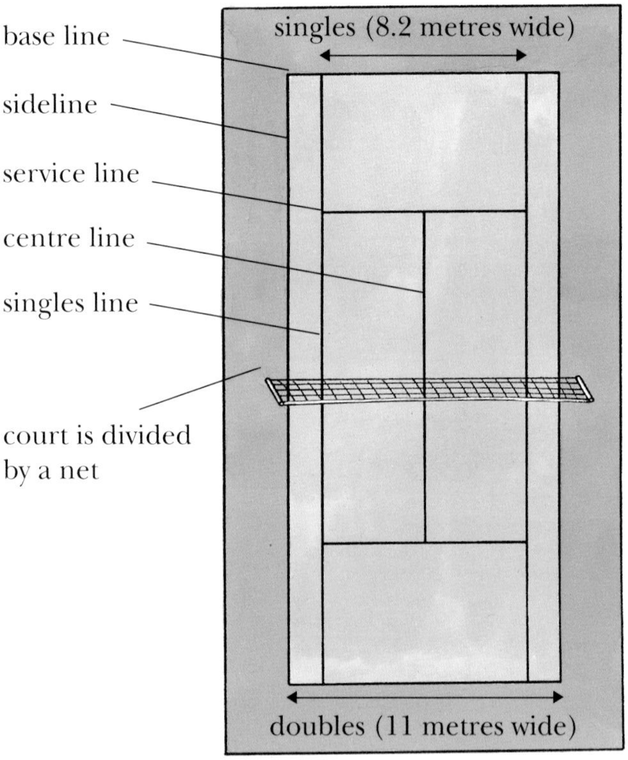

EQUIPMENT

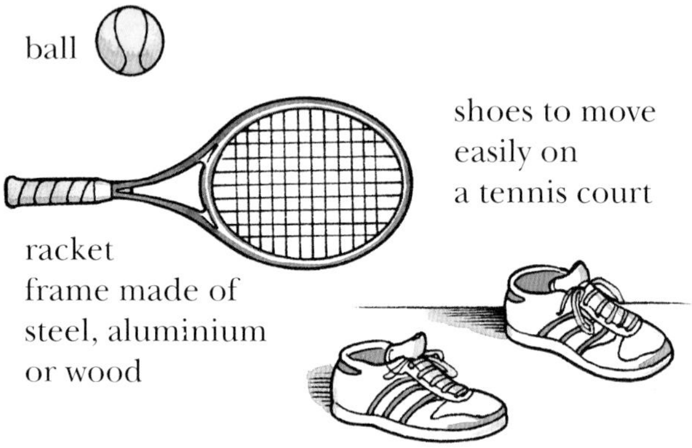

HOW TO PLAY TENNIS ▼

- A tennis match is played with two or four players.
- A player hits the ball over the net with a racket. The player at the other end of the court hits the ball back.
- Each player tries to hit the ball so the player at the other end cannot hit it back over the net.

SCORING

A player scores a point when the other player cannot hit the ball back over the net, or when the ball is hit back but lands outside the court.

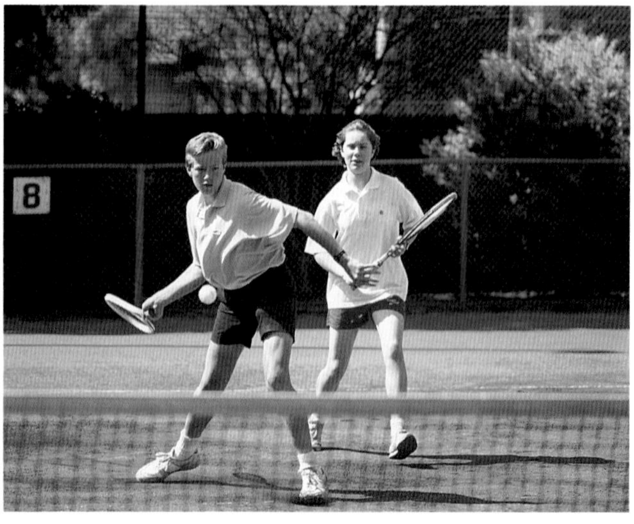

SINGLES AND DOUBLES

A singles match is when two people play. A doubles match is when four people play.

TIDES

SEE ALSO • Gravity • Moon • Seashore Life

Tides are the rise and fall of the sea level. There are two high tides and two low tides each day.

HOW TIDES ARE CAUSED

Tides happen because of the pull of the Moon and the Sun on the oceans of the Earth. The pull is caused by gravity.

HIGH TIDE AND LOW TIDE

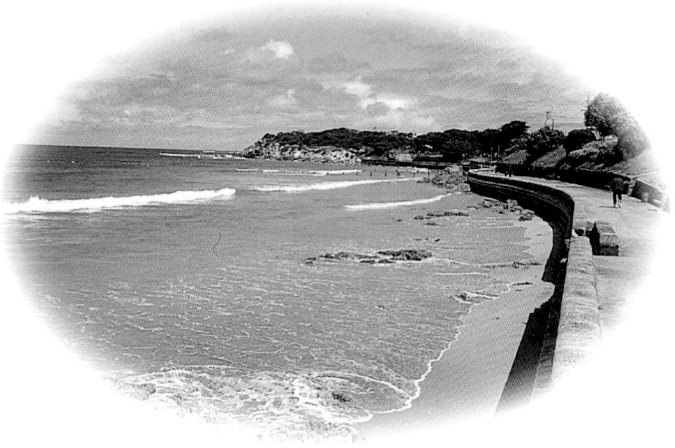

High tide is when the water is high on the shore.

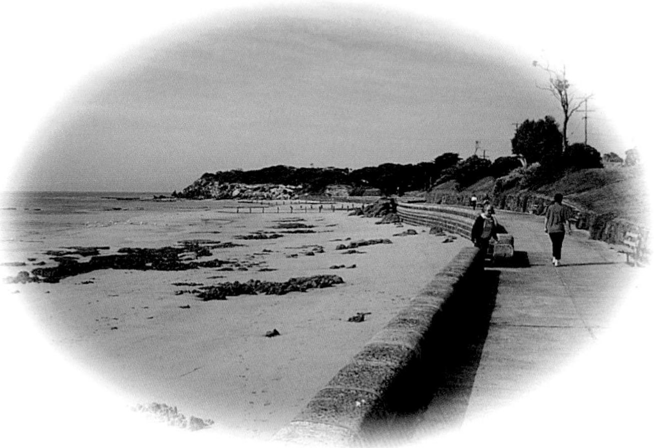

Low tide is when the water is low on the shore.

SPRING TIDES

Spring tides are the biggest tides. They happen when the Moon and the Sun are pulling together on the same side of the Earth.

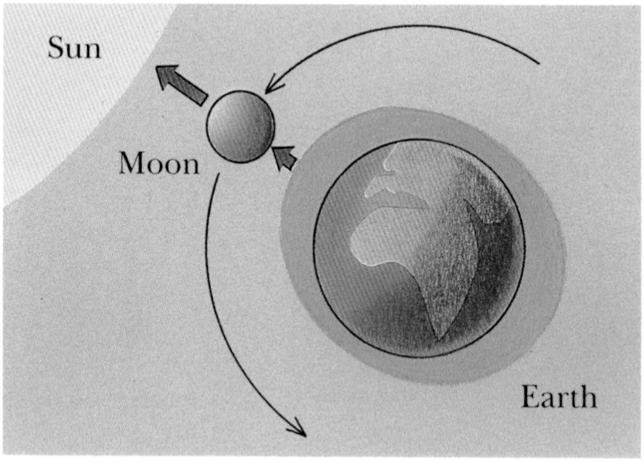

NEAP TIDES

Neap tides are the smallest tides. They happen when the Moon and the Sun are pulling at right angles to each other.

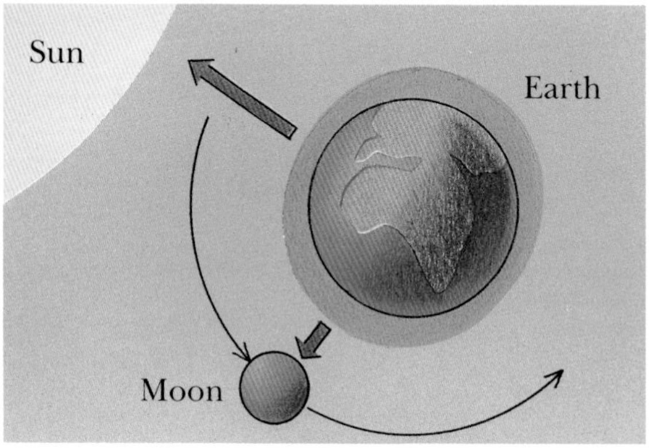

TORCH

SEE ALSO • Electricity • Light

A torch is a portable light. Batteries inside the torch produce an electric current. The electric current lights the bulb.

HOW A TORCH WORKS

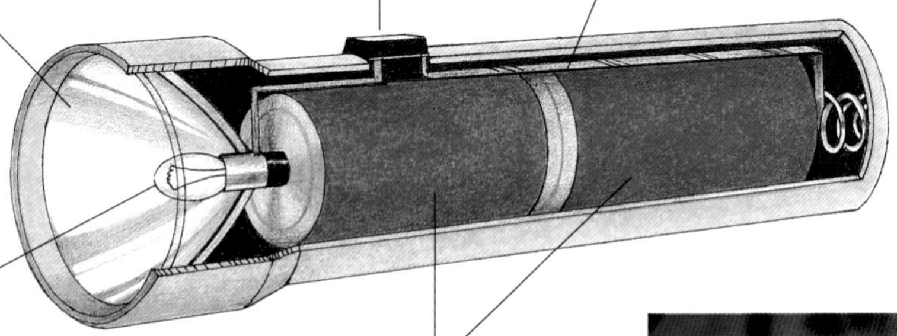

INTERESTING FACT

Many batteries can be recharged using solar power and other generators. Batteries can be recycled.

Batteries produce an electric current that flows one way around a circuit. When the switch is turned on, the circuit is complete. The top of the battery is connected to the bulb.

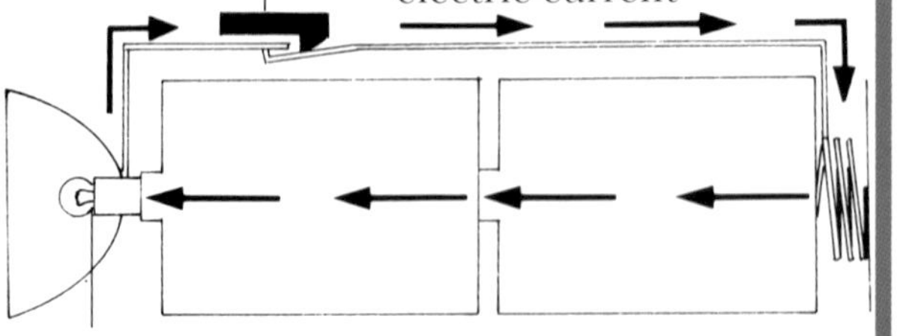

Torches are useful outdoors at night. ▶

TOY

SEE ALSO • Doll • Games • Kite • Puppet

A toy is something you play with.
You can have lots of fun playing with toys.

HISTORY

Long ago, children played with a big iron hoop and a stick. They ran along beside the hoop and kept it moving with a stick.

INTERESTING FACT

Teddy bears were first made in 1902 in the USA. They were named after President Theodore 'Teddy' Roosevelt.

TOYS HELP YOU LEARN

- Construction toys help ▶ you learn about design and building.
- Young children can learn to count with building blocks. They can also learn about balance.
- Toys are fun to share. Children learn to cooperate when they play together. ▼

TRAIN

SEE ALSO • Transport

A train is a kind of carriage that moves on a railway. Trains carry people and goods from one place to another. Engines pull the train carriages along the railway.

PARTS OF AN ELECTRIC TRAIN

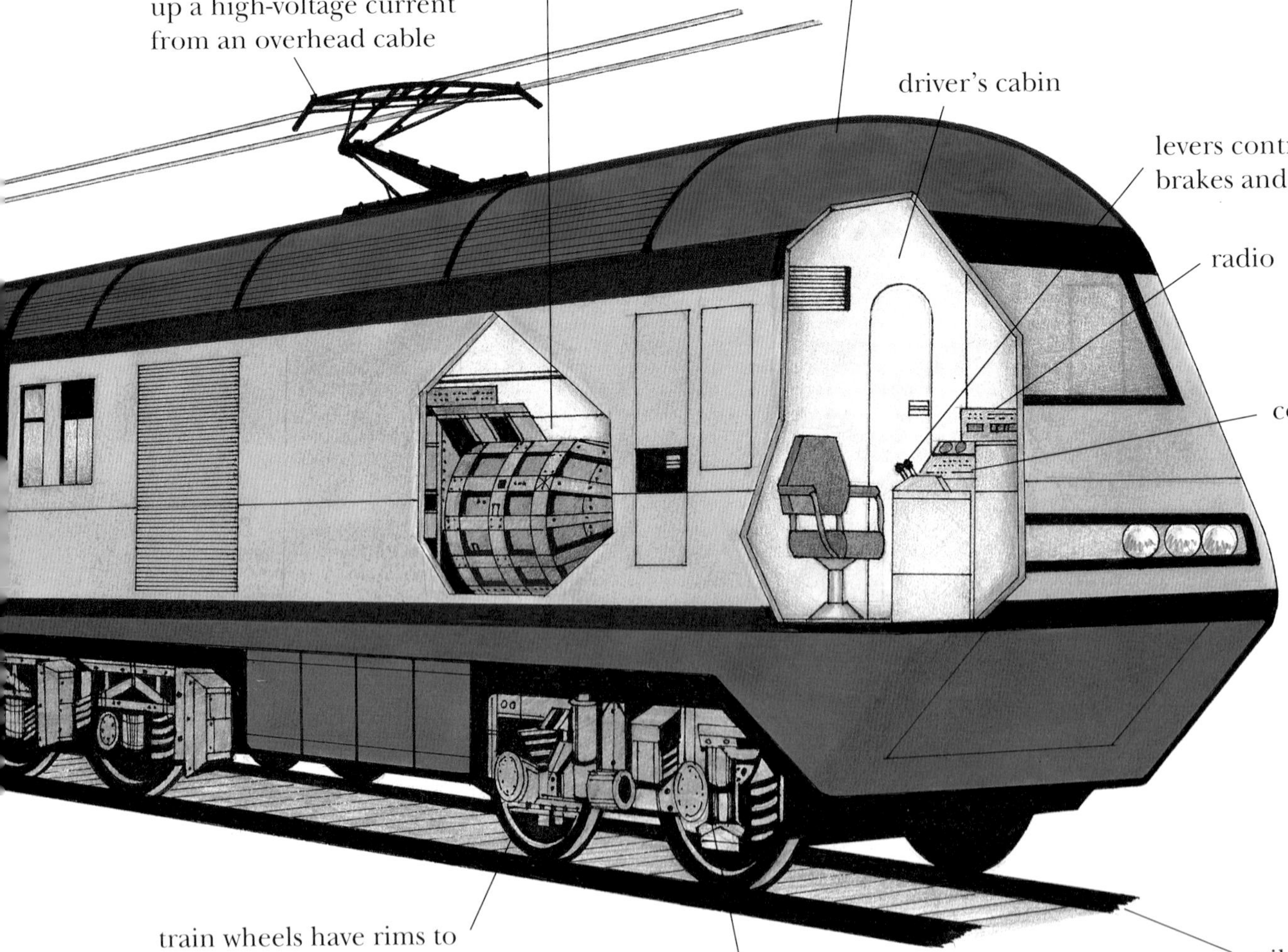

STEAM ENGINES

The first trains were pulled by steam engines. In the engine room, coal was burned to produce steam which powered the engine.

COMFORTABLE TRAINS

Many trains travel long distances. They have sleeping and eating carriages.

MODERN TRAIN CABINS

Train drivers use computers and radios to control the speed and brakes of a train, to check faults and to keep in touch with signalling centres.

SUBWAY TRAINS

Subway or underground trains run along railways in tunnels under the ground.

FUTURE TRANSPORT

Trains could be the best transport for the future. They use less fuel and cause less pollution than cars and trucks. They can carry lots of people and large loads of goods.

MONORAIL ▲ TRAINS

Monorail trains are electric trains that run on a single rail above the traffic. Some monorail trains hang from the single rail.

TRANSPORT

SEE ALSO • Aeroplane • Bicycle • Motor Car • Road • Ship • Truck

Transport is a way of carrying people and goods from one place to another. Some kinds of transport move on land, some travel across water and some travel in the air.

HISTORY

• Long ago, people walked from place to place. They carried everything themselves.

• Then people started to use animals to carry goods and to move from place to place. Animals were a faster way of transport.

• In the 1800s, people used stagecoaches pulled by horses to move around.

LAND TRANSPORT

Cars, buses, trucks, bicycles and trains can carry people and goods on land.

Cars are the most popular kind of private transport.

Bicycles are a clean and cheap way of getting around.

Buses can carry many passengers from place to place.

Trucks and lorries use roads and motorways to carry goods.

WATER TRANSPORT

There are many different kinds of water transport.

Rafts were the earliest kind of sea transport.

Sailing ships use the wind to move.

Steam ships are faster than sailing ships. Coal is burnt to drive their engines.

Modern ships can provide quick transport for passengers and goods.

AIR TRANSPORT

Today, the quickest way to travel is by air.

Hot-air balloons were the first kind of air transport.

Today, millions of people travel by aeroplane. Aeroplanes also carry mail and goods.

POLLUTION

Most kinds of transport burn fuel for power. This creates dangerous gases that pollute the air. Walking, cycling and roller-skating are ways of travelling that do not create pollution.

Trains run on steel tracks.

SPACECRAFT ▶

Astronauts travel in spacecraft into space.

INTERESTING FACT

Land vehicles can travel across rivers on bridges and under the sea in tunnels.

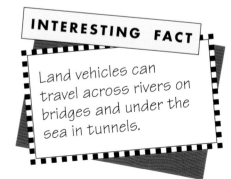

TREE

SEE ALSO • Forest • Fruit • Leaf • Nut • Plant • Rain Forest

A tree is a large plant. Trees have a trunk, branches and leaves. Trees take in carbon dioxide from the air and provide us with oxygen.

PARTS OF A TREE

Trees:
- act as windbreaks
- protect animals and crops.

Height: Most trees grow to between 4.5 and 6 metres tall

Leaves:
- take in carbon dioxide
- give off oxygen
- provide food for animals and insects
- shelter animals from wind and rain, and provide shade.

Flowers, fruit and nuts:
- attract insects and insect-eating birds
- provide food for people, animals and birds.

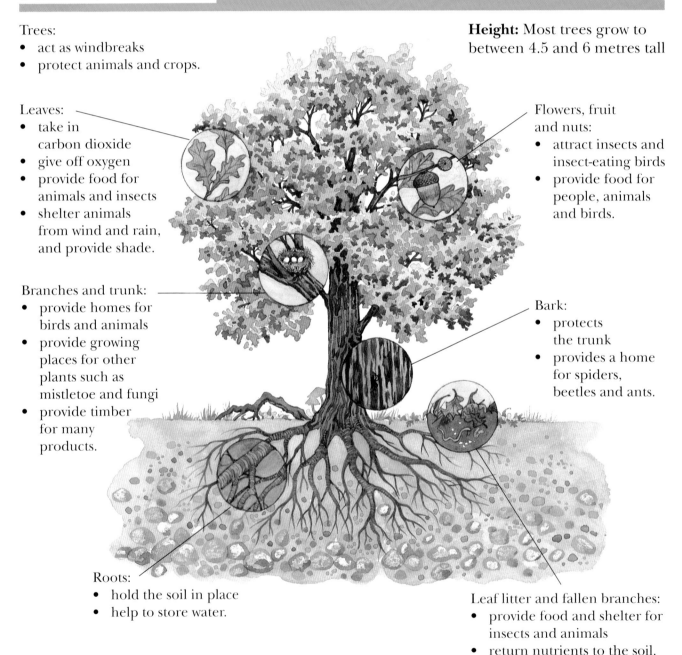

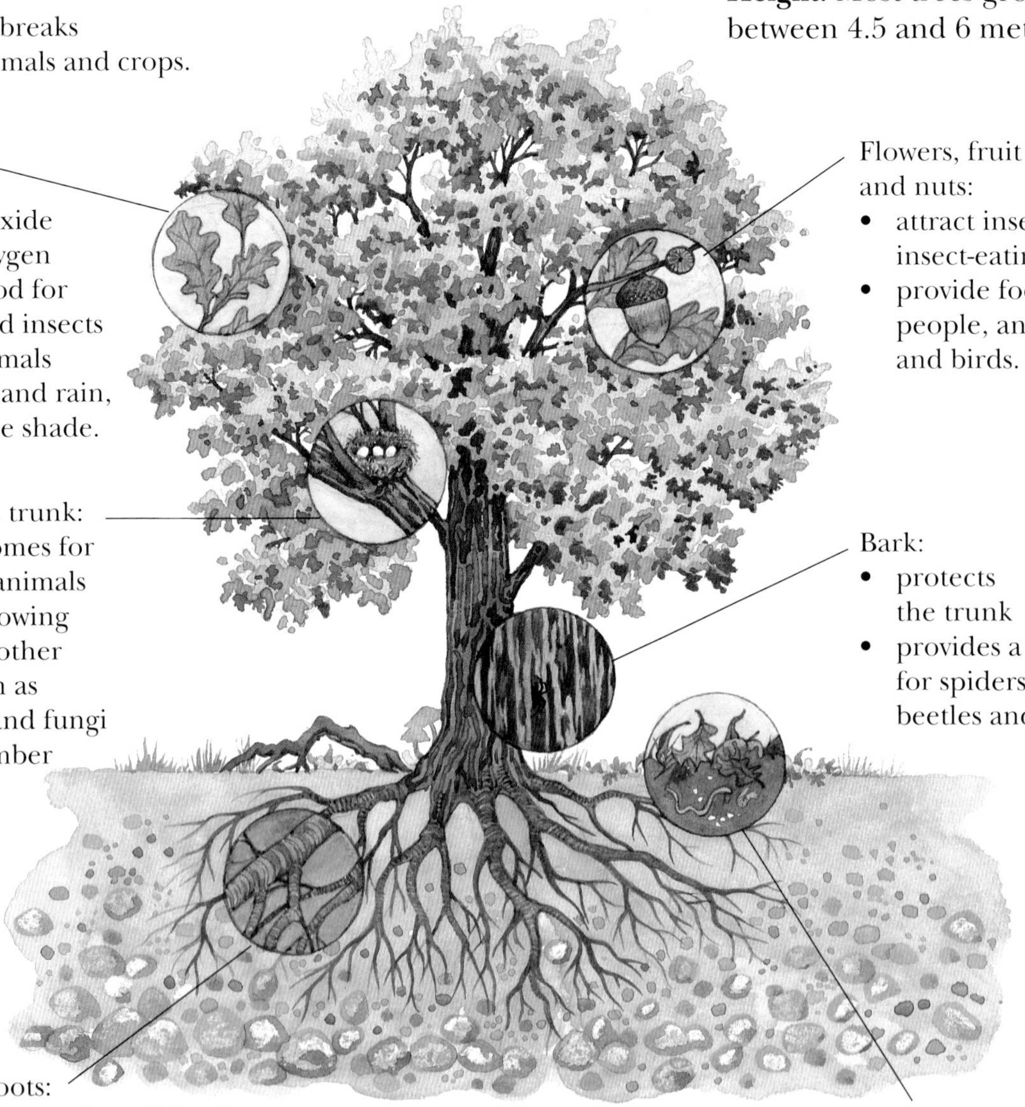

Branches and trunk:
- provide homes for birds and animals
- provide growing places for other plants such as mistletoe and fungi
- provide timber for many products.

Bark:
- protects the trunk
- provides a home for spiders, beetles and ants.

Roots:
- hold the soil in place
- help to store water.

Leaf litter and fallen branches:
- provide food and shelter for insects and animals
- return nutrients to the soil.

KINDS OF TREES

There are two main kinds of trees – conifer trees and broad-leafed trees.

Conifer trees produce cones instead of flowers.

- Some conifers such as fir trees have long, needle-shaped leaves. Others such as the cypress tree have triangular leaves.
- Most conifers keep their leaves all year round. They are called evergreen trees.

▶

Broad-leafed trees produce flowers. ▲

- Broad-leafed trees usually have wide, flat leaves.
- Most broad-leafed trees are deciduous. They shed their leaves in the autumn.

USEFUL PRODUCTS FROM TREES

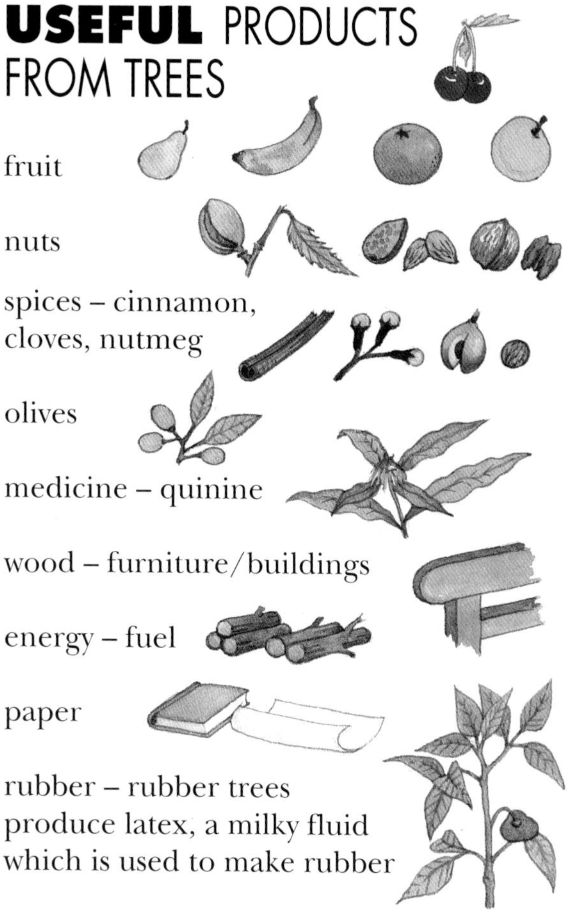

REST AND RELAXATION

Trees give us shelter and shade during the hot summer.

TRUCK

SEE ALSO • Bridge • Motor Car • Road • Train • Transport

A truck is a large vehicle which is used to carry heavy loads. Trucks travel on roads and highways. Some trucks are built to carry special loads such as fuel. Trucks are sometimes called lorries.

PARTS OF A MODERN TRUCK

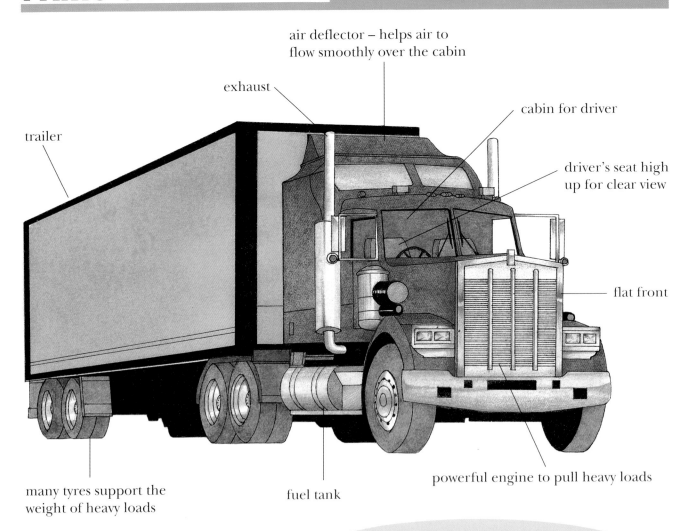

Many large modern trucks are articulated. Articulated trucks have segments. Joints between each segment help the truck to move easily along the road.

KINDS OF TRUCKS

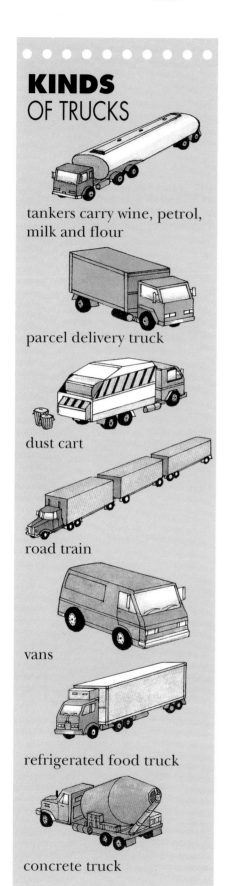

tankers carry wine, petrol, milk and flour

parcel delivery truck

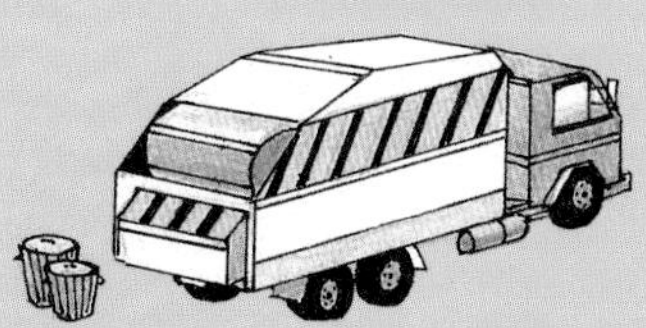

dust cart

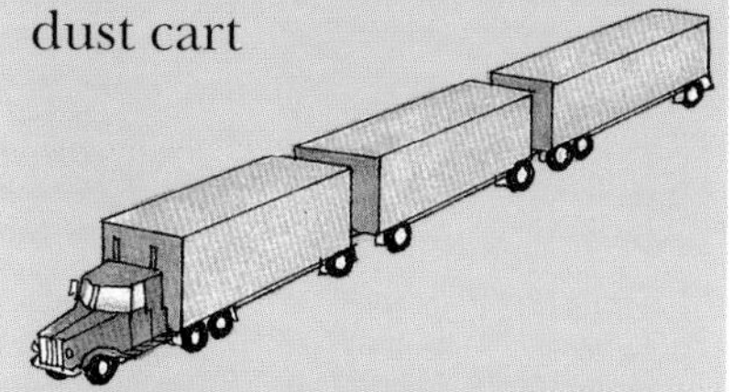

road train

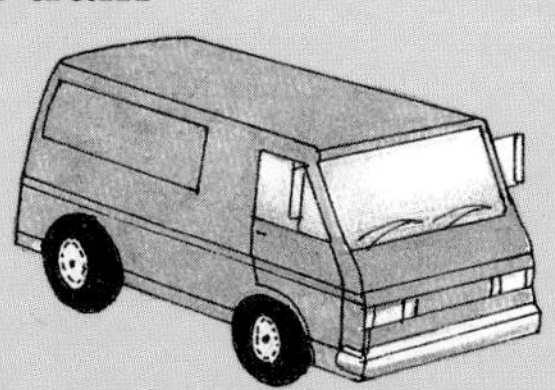

vans

refrigerated food truck

concrete truck

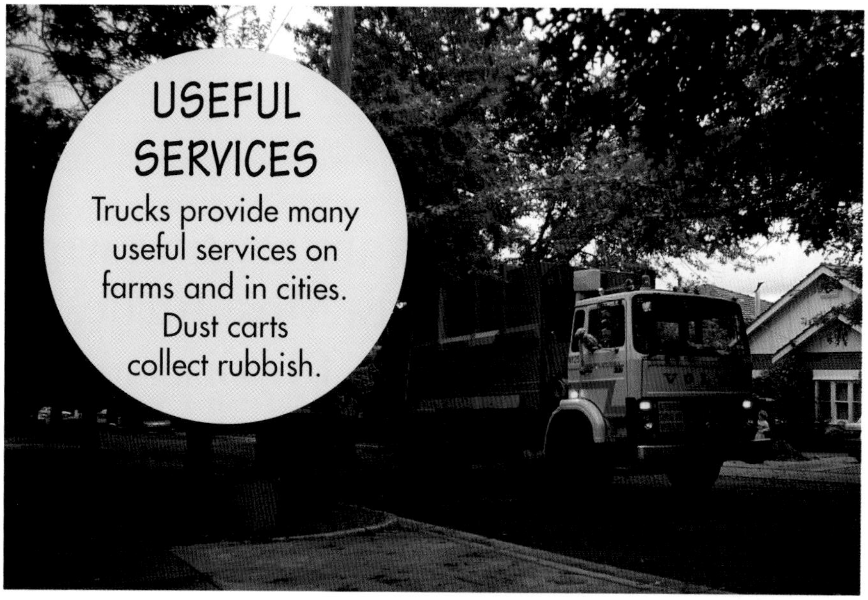

USEFUL SERVICES

Trucks provide many useful services on farms and in cities. Dust carts collect rubbish.

BUILDING SITE ▶ TRUCKS

Some trucks bring concrete to building sites. The drum turns so the concrete stays soft. The concrete is poured from the mixer.

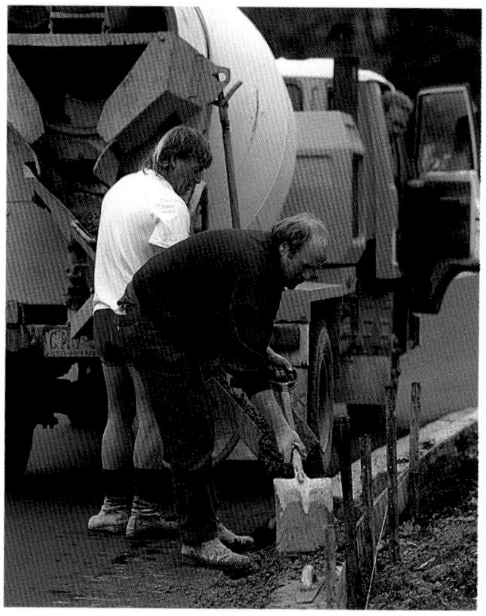

RELIEF ▼ TRUCKS

Trucks are often used to deliver food and medical supplies to places that are cut off from other forms of transport.

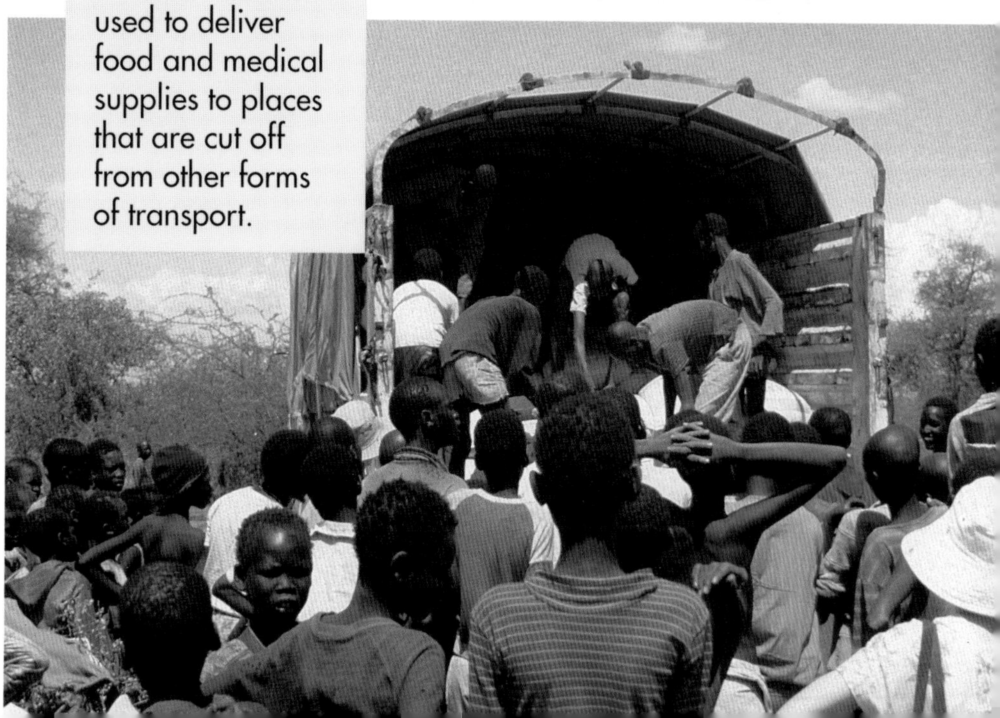

TURTLES AND TORTOISES

SEE ALSO • Animal • Endangered Species • Reptiles

Turtles and tortoises are reptiles which have a shell. They move very slowly. Most turtles live in water and have legs like flippers. Tortoises usually live on land or in fresh water.

PARTS OF A SEA TURTLE

Length: up to 2 metres
Weight: up to 500 kilograms

INTERESTING FACT

Turtles look the same today as they did 176 million years ago.

WHERE TURTLES LIVE

Most turtles and tortoises live in the warmer parts of the world.

FOOD

seaweed or sea grass

water plants

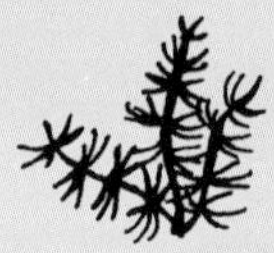

small sea and water animals

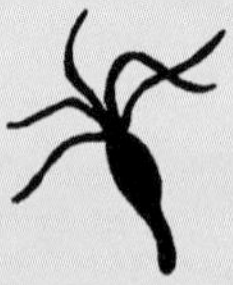

jellyfish

tadpoles

shellfish – crabs

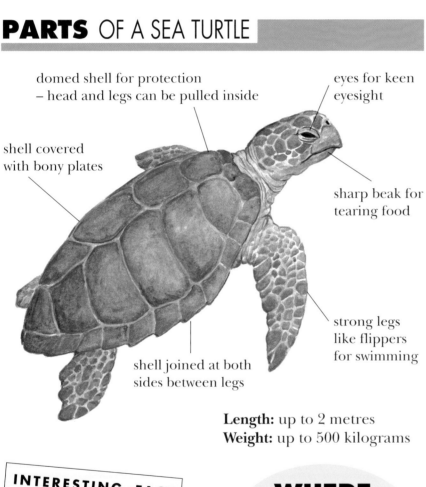

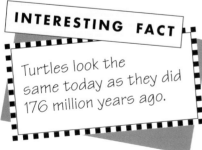

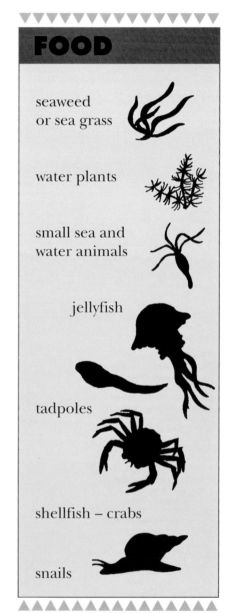

snails

HOW TURTLES LIVE

- Turtles spend most of their lives at sea. They come ashore to breed.
- The female turtle digs a hole in the sand or soil in which to lay her eggs. About two months later, the eggs hatch.
- The hatchlings make their own way to the sea.

INTERESTING FACT

Some turtles can live for more than 100 years.

KINDS OF TURTLES AND TORTOISES

Marine or sea turtles spend most of their lives in the sea. Many sea turtles, such as the green sea turtle, have webbed feet or feet like flippers to help them swim. Some marine turtles can swim as fast as 35 kilometres per hour.
▶

Today there are few giant tortoises left. Many have been hunted by people and animals that have been brought into the area. Giant land tortoises live on islands in the Pacific and Indian Oceans.
▼

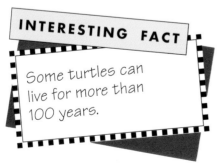

Terrapins are small turtles. They belong to the family of turtles that live on land and in fresh water.
◀

UNGULATES

SEE ALSO • Animal • Grassland • Mammal

Ungulates are mammals with hooves. All ungulates are plant-eating animals (herbivores).

KINDS OF UNGULATES

There are two kinds of ungulates.

- Some ungulates have hooves with an even number of toes. Most ungulates have two toes on each foot. Some have four toes but most of the weight is carried on two toes.

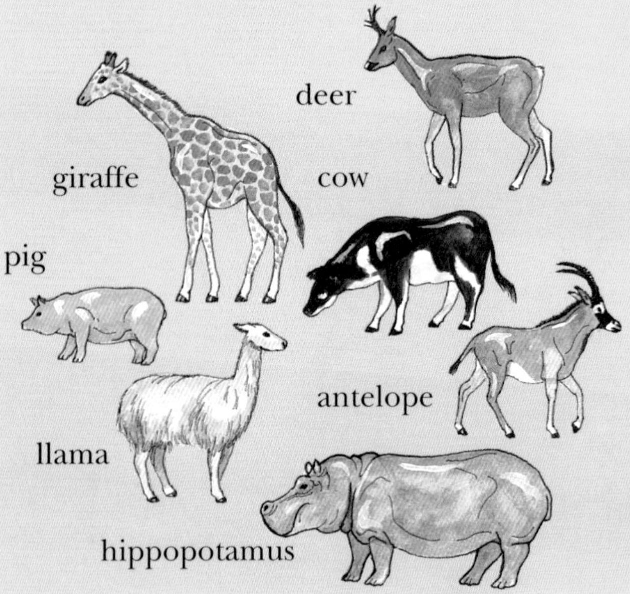

- Some ungulates have an odd number of toes on each foot. They have either one toe or three toes. They usually carry their weight on the middle toe of each foot.

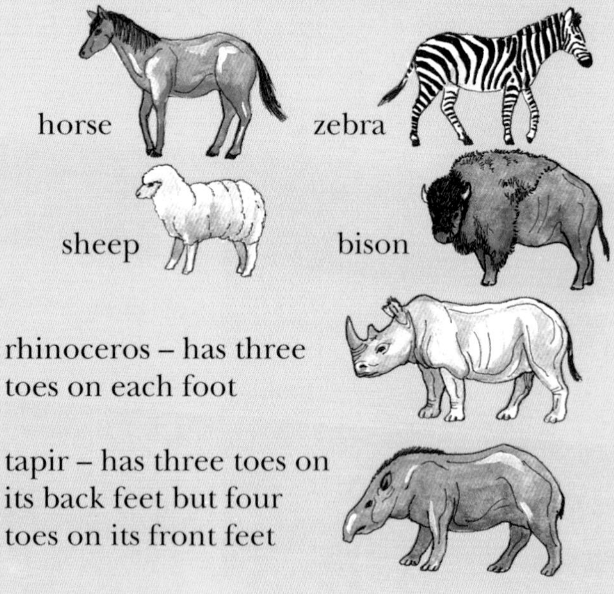

◀ LLAMAS

Ungulates such as llamas roam in search of food. They live mainly on open grassland. Most ungulates can run fast to escape enemies.

UNITED NATIONS

SEE ALSO • Continent • Flag

The United Nations is a group of about 150 nations that work together to prevent wars. The United Nations was set up in 1945, at the end of the Second World War.

THE UNITED NATIONS SYMBOL

The symbol is a map of the world with olive branches.

UNICEF ▼

The United Nations International Children's Education Fund was formed to help children who suffered during the Second World War. Today, UNICEF provides education, health care and medical help for children around the world.

PEACE-KEEPING FORCE

The United Nations sends peace-keeping forces to some countries to prevent war.

The United Nations headquarters is in New York City, USA.

UNIVERSE

SEE ALSO • Astronomy • Galaxy • Meteor • Planet • Star • Sun

The Universe is all the stars, planets, moons and other bodies in space. Earth is one planet in the Universe. No one knows how big the Universe is or if it ends.

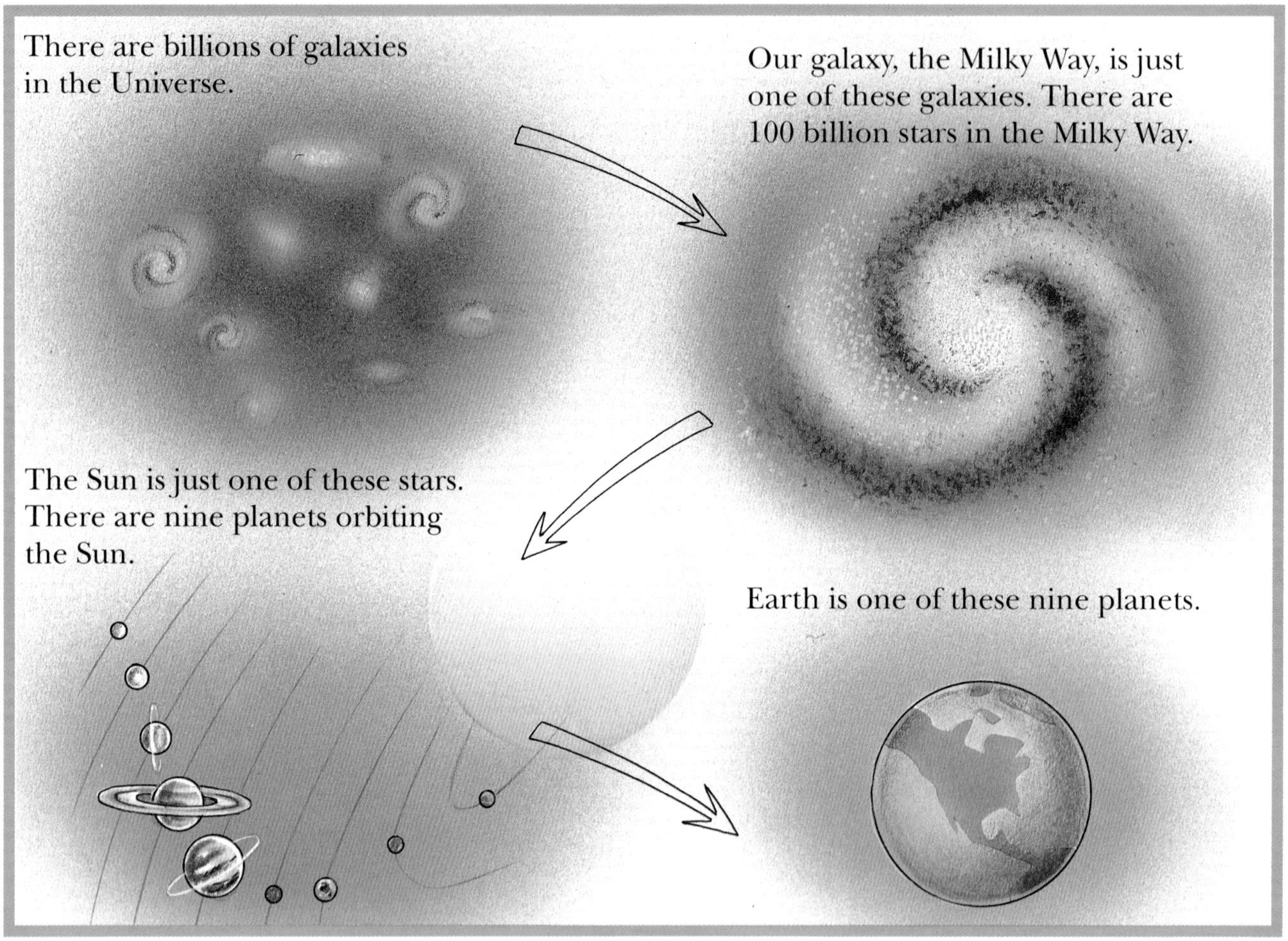
There are billions of galaxies in the Universe.
Our galaxy, the Milky Way, is just one of these galaxies. There are 100 billion stars in the Milky Way.
The Sun is just one of these stars. There are nine planets orbiting the Sun.
Earth is one of these nine planets.

THE EXPANDING UNIVERSE

All the galaxies in the Universe are travelling away from each other, as the Universe expands. The galaxies move away from each other in much the same way as spots on a balloon move apart when the balloon is blown up.

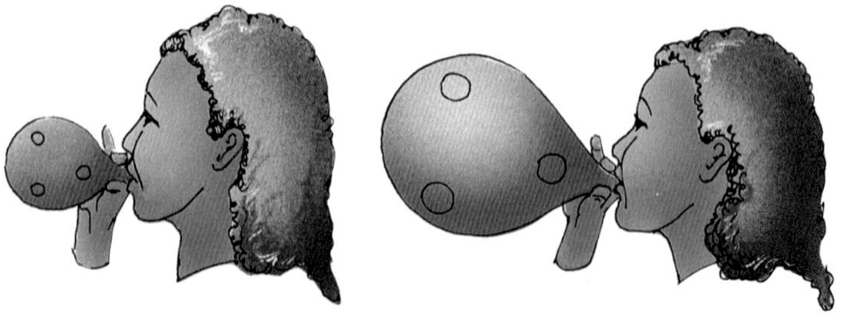

VEGETABLE

SEE ALSO • Flower • Food • Fruit • Garden • Nut • Plant

A vegetable is a plant or part of a plant you can eat. The leaves, roots, flowers or stems of a plant can be a vegetable.

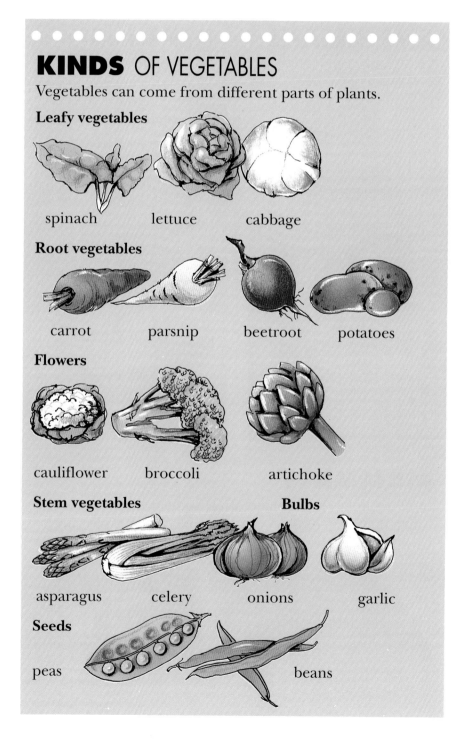

KINDS OF VEGETABLES

Vegetables can come from different parts of plants.

Leafy vegetables

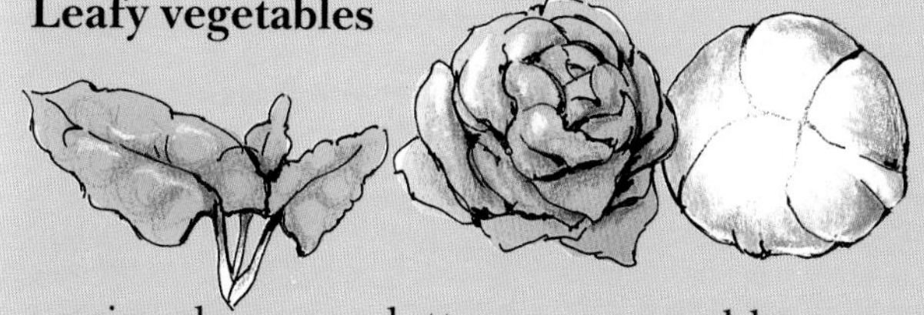

spinach lettuce cabbage

Root vegetables

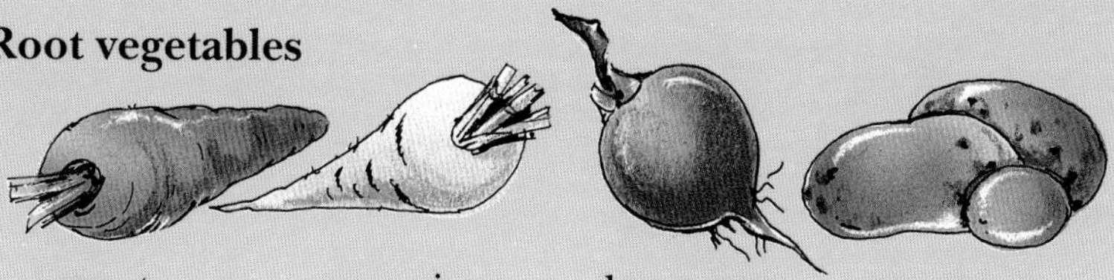

carrot parsnip beetroot potatoes

Flowers

cauliflower broccoli artichoke

Stem vegetables **Bulbs**

asparagus celery onions garlic

Seeds

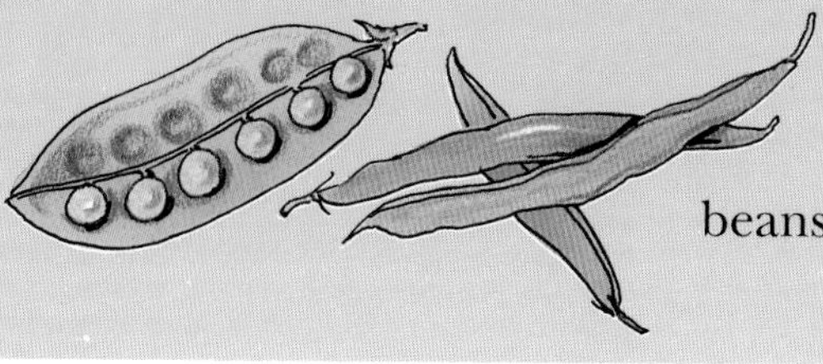

peas beans

VEGETABLE MARKETS

Vegetables are grown on farms. Farmers sell their produce at markets.

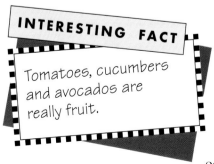

RAW OR COOKED

Vegetables can be eaten raw or cooked. A salad is a mixture of raw vegetables.

INTERESTING FACT

Tomatoes, cucumbers and avocados are really fruit.

VERTEBRATE

SEE ALSO • Amphibians • Bird • Fish • Mammal • Reptiles

A vertebrate is an animal with a backbone. There are many different kinds of vertebrates. They are divided into five main groups.

FISH

Fish live in water. They have scaly bodies.

AMPHIBIANS

Amphibians can live in water or on land. They have moist skin.

REPTILES

Most reptiles live on land, but some live in water. They have dry, scaly bodies.

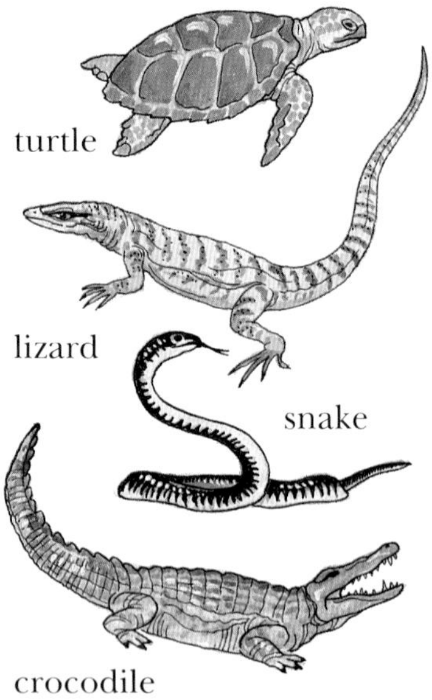

BIRDS

All birds have feathers and most are able to fly. The ostrich, emu, penguin and kiwi cannot fly.

MAMMALS

Most mammals live on land, while some live in water. All mammals feed their young on milk. Their bodies are usually covered with hair or fur.

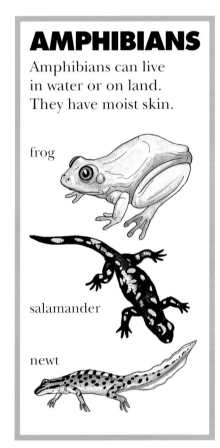

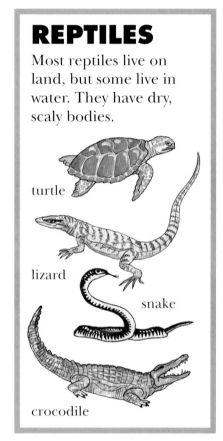

VETERINARIAN

SEE ALSO • Animal • Doctor • Farming • Pet • Zoo

A veterinarian is an animal doctor. Veterinarians are usually called vets. They treat animals to keep them healthy. Animals are difficult to treat because they cannot say where it hurts.

CITY VETS

City vets usually treat pets such as cats, dogs, birds, goldfish and other more unusual pets.

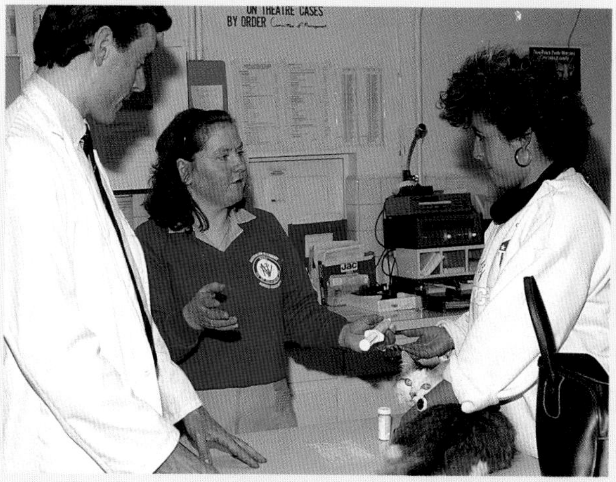

COUNTRY VETS ▲

Country vets treat farm animals. Vets give animals injections to protect them from disease.

◀ OPERATING ON ANIMALS

Vets often have to operate on animals. Large animals have operations on a table that can be tilted.

VITAMINS

SEE ALSO • Digestion • Food • Fruit • Vegetable

Vitamins are chemicals our bodies need to grow and stay healthy. We get vitamins from food and sunlight. There are six kinds of vitamins.

A HEALTHY DIET

Vitamins are used in tiny quantities in our bodies. A varied diet provides all the vitamins we need.

VITAMIN A

Vitamin A is used for growth, and to keep our skin and eyes healthy. It is found in oily fish, carrots, spinach, liver and dairy products.

B VITAMINS

B vitamins are used for healthy growth, to help release energy from our food and to keep our skin healthy. They are found mainly in cereals, leafy vegetables, liver, eggs and milk.

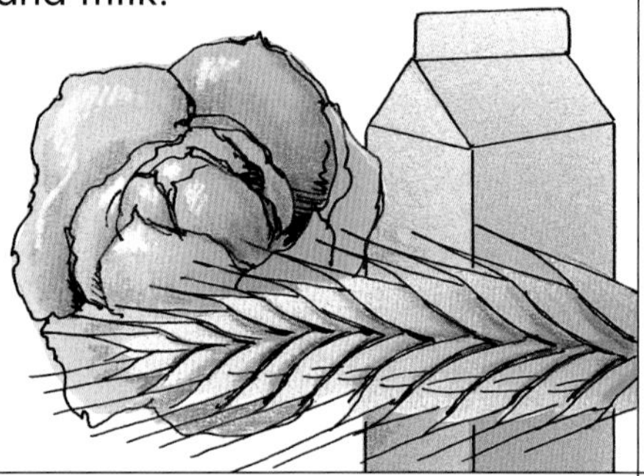

VITAMIN C

Vitamin C is used to keep our blood and gums healthy, and to prevent colds. Vitamin C cannot be stored in the body. We need Vitamin C every day. It is found in fresh fruit and vegetables.

VITAMIN D

Vitamin D is used to keep our bones and teeth healthy. It is found mostly in oily fish, eggs and dairy products. It is also made in small amounts by sun on the skin.

VITAMIN E

Vitamin E is used for cell growth and to heal wounds. It is found in many foods, especially cereals and green leafy vegetables.

VITAMIN K

Vitamin K is used to help blood clot which stops the loss of blood from wounds. It is found in green vegetables.

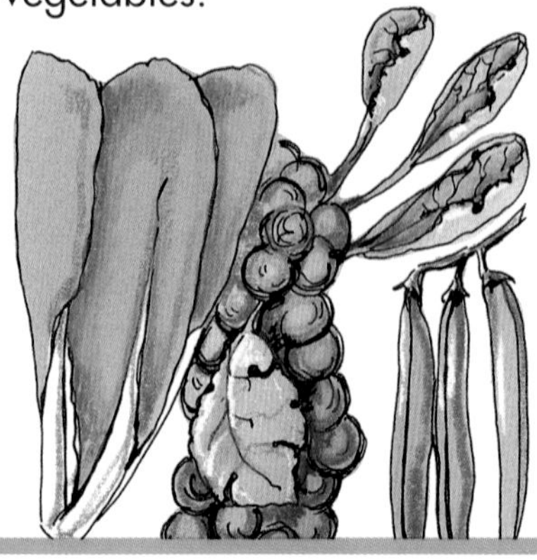

VOLCANO

SEE ALSO • Earth • Earthquake • Island • Lake • Mountain

A volcano is a hole in the Earth's crust. Sometimes lava, burning gas and ash erupt through this hole.

HOW A VOLCANO IS MADE

- Red-hot liquid rock lies under the Earth's crust.
- When the pressure of the molten rocks and gases builds up, they explode through the centre of the volcano. The explosion is called an eruption.

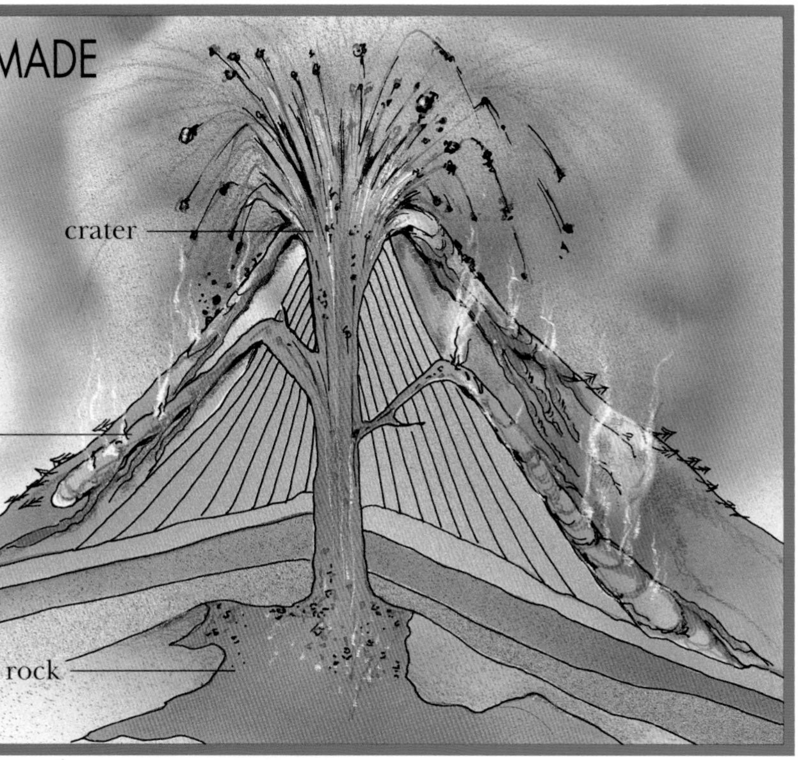

ACTIVE VOLCANOES ▼

Some volcanoes erupt. Scientists can give warnings of possible eruptions.

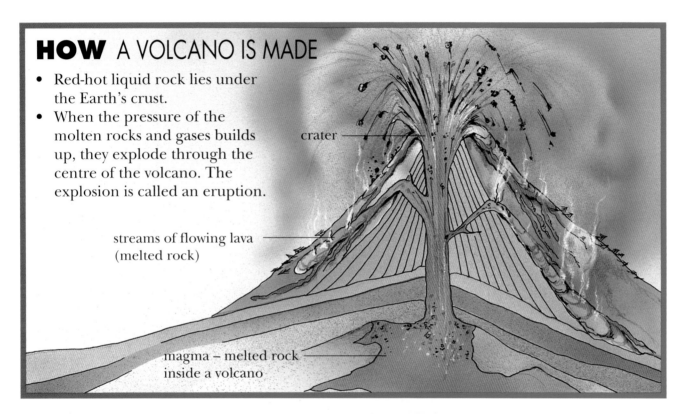

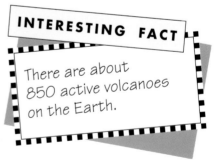

INTERESTING FACT

There are about 850 active volcanoes on the Earth.

◀ Many volcanoes form cone-shaped mountains. The lava cools and hardens into rock.

VULTURE

SEE ALSO • Animal • Bird

A vulture is a large bird of prey. Vultures eat the remains of dead animals (carrion). They help to stop diseases spreading.

PARTS OF A BLACK VULTURE

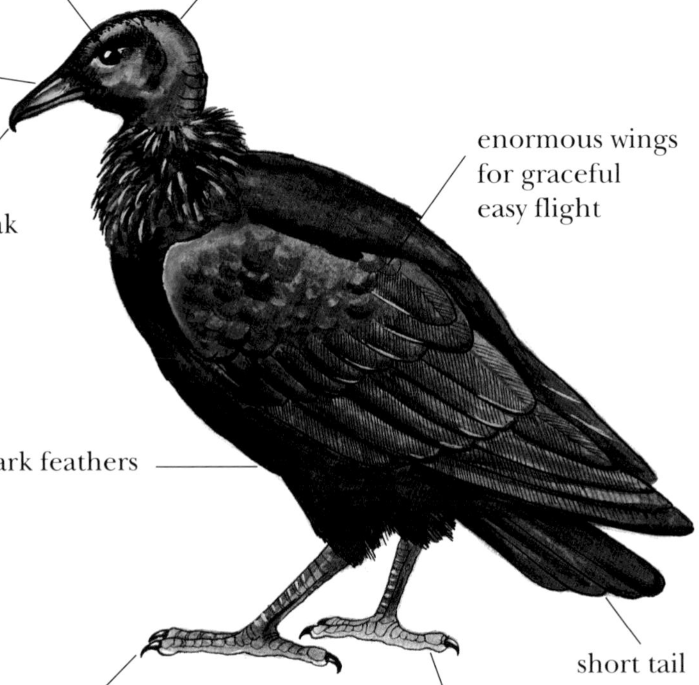

Length: up to 110 centimetres
Wingspan: 2.5 metres

KINDS OF VULTURES

- New World vultures feed on dead animals.
- Old World vultures belong to the hawk family. They feed on living animals and carrion. They have a stronger beak, and stronger and larger feet and talons than New World vultures.

INTERESTING FACT

Vultures, owls, falcons, hawks and eagles are birds of prey. They are also called raptors.

WHERE VULTURES LIVE

New World vultures
- ● North America
- ■ South America

Old World vultures
- ◆ Europe
- ★ Asia
- ▲ Africa

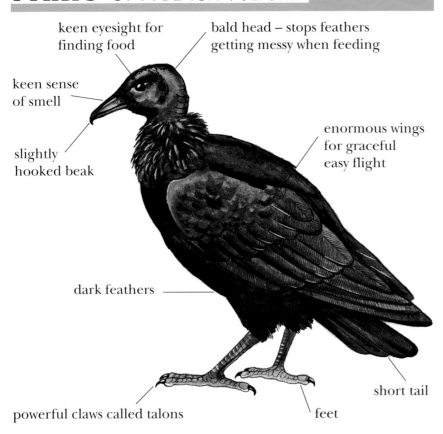

FOOD

New World vultures
carrion – remains of dead animals

Old World vultures

small animals

carrion

The condor is a New World vulture. It is the largest bird in South America. It has a wingspan of three metres.

HOW VULTURES MOVE

Vultures are graceful fliers. They circle in the sky and drop suddenly to the ground when they find food.

HOW VULTURES LIVE

- Vultures live in large flocks, except during the breeding season.
- During the breeding season, vultures pair off. They nest on cliffs or in logs or caves.
- The female lays one to three eggs. When the eggs hatch, the parents feed the young vultures.

The lammergeyer or bearded vulture is an Old World vulture. It eats bone marrow. It drops bones from high in the air until they break. ▼

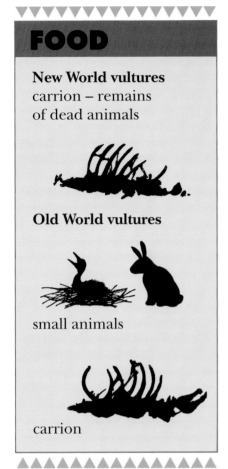

WATER

SEE ALSO • Glacier • Lake • Ocean • Pollution • Rain • River

Water is a liquid. It has no colour, taste or smell. People, animals and plants all need water to stay alive.

THE WATER CYCLE

The Earth's water is always moving, from the sea to the air to the land.

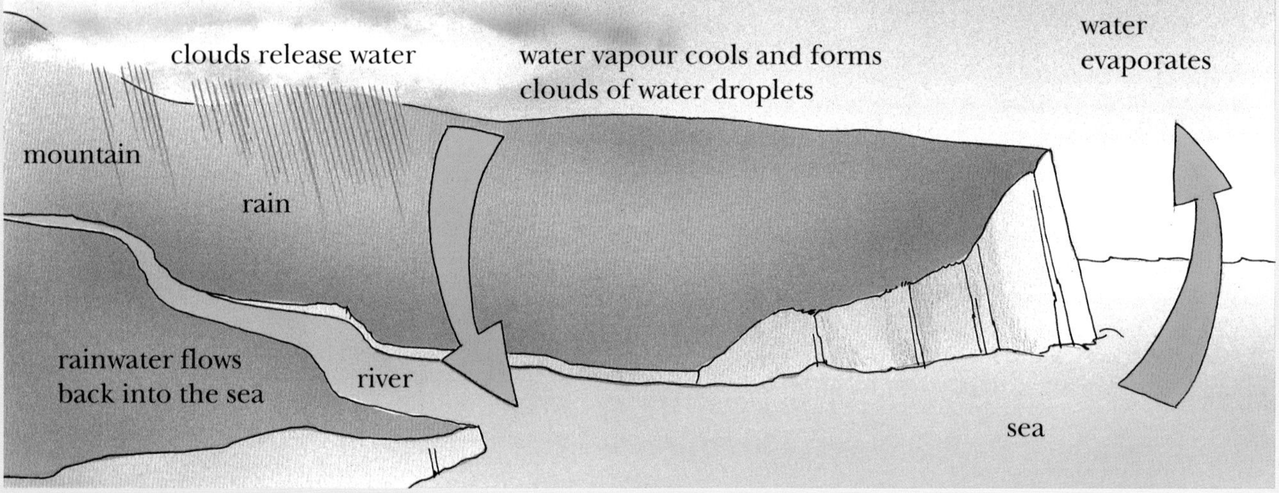

SALT AND FRESH WATER

Water covers 70 per cent of the Earth's surface.

- Salt water in the oceans makes up 97 per cent of the Earth's water.
- Only three per cent of the Earth's water is fresh water. Fresh water comes from rain, snow and melting glaciers. It is found in rivers, lakes, ponds and streams. It is also found underground.

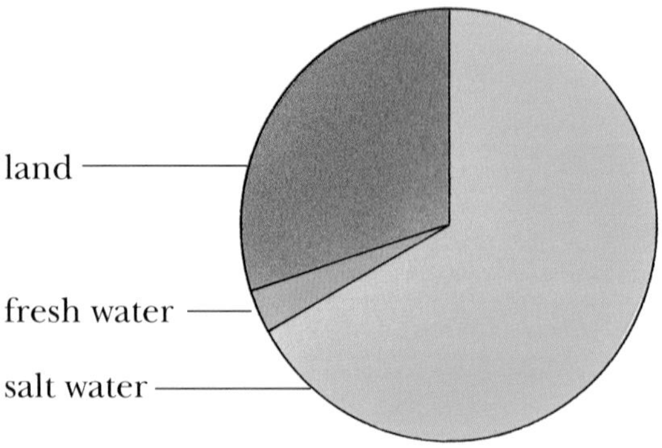

WATER CAN BE SOLID, LIQUID OR GAS

- Ice is solid water. Ice forms when water is cooled to zero degrees Celsius.
- Rain is liquid water. The water in your tap and in the rivers and oceans is also liquid water.
- Steam is water as a gas. Steam forms when water is heated to 100 degrees Celsius.

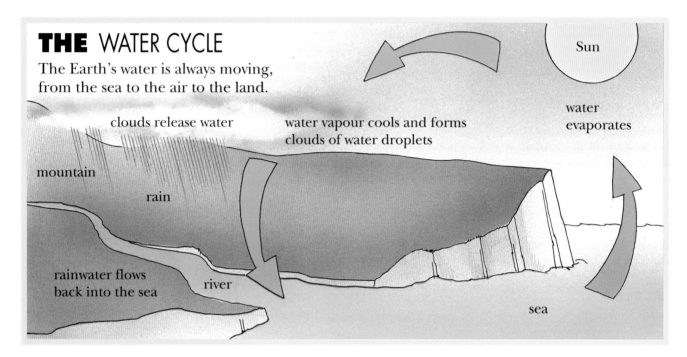

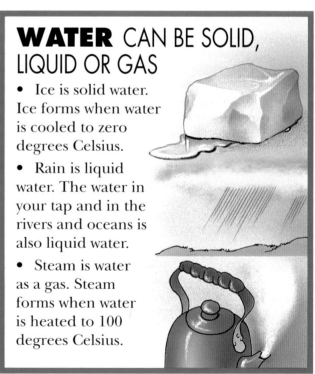

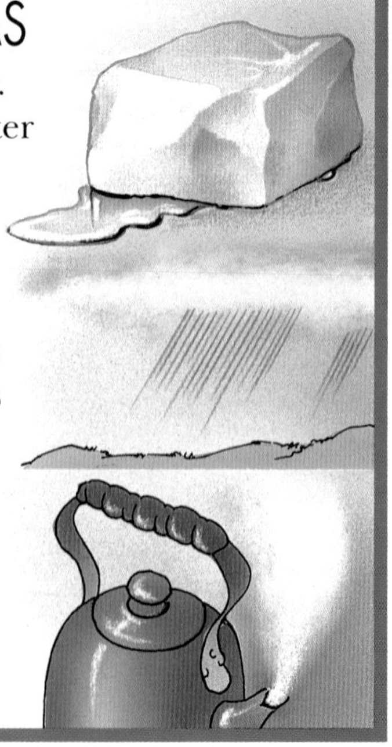

WATER SUPPLY ▲

Most of the water we use comes from rivers. Water is stored in reservoirs and dams. It is treated to remove bacteria and other things that can harm us.

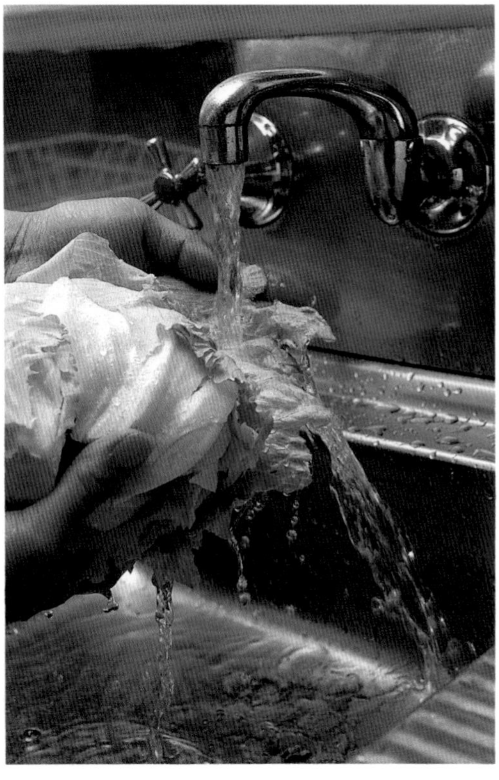

WATER FOR THE WORLD

In some countries, clean water is pumped from reservoirs into homes. You just have to turn on a tap.

In other countries, water is scarce. People have to walk long distances to the nearest well to fetch water.

USES OF WATER

Water is used every day.

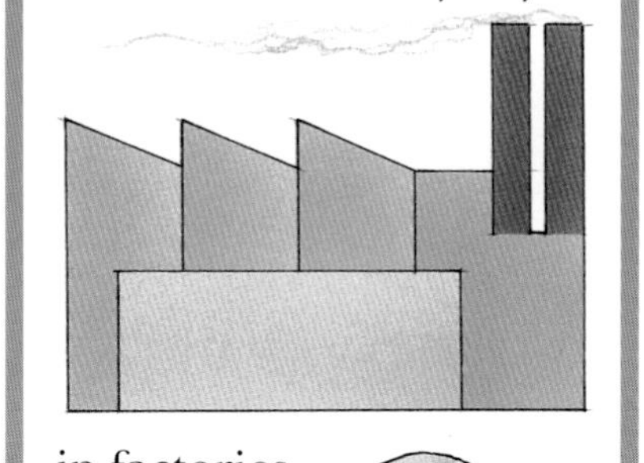

in factories

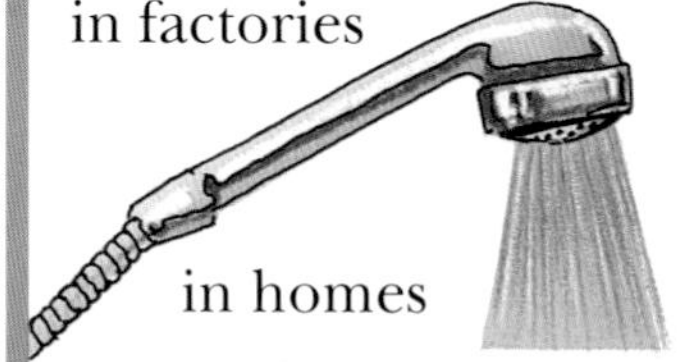

in homes

on farms

for transport

for power

for relaxation and sport

INTERESTING FACT

The human body is 65 per cent water.

WATERFALL

SEE ALSO • Mountain • River • Water

A waterfall is a river that falls over a ledge or cliff. Some waterfalls have little water flowing down them. Others have great amounts of water plunging down.

HOW A WATERFALL IS MADE

Waterfalls are usually made as a river flows over bands of soft and hard rock in the river bed. Over thousands of years, the soft rock is worn away, leaving a cliff of hard rock.

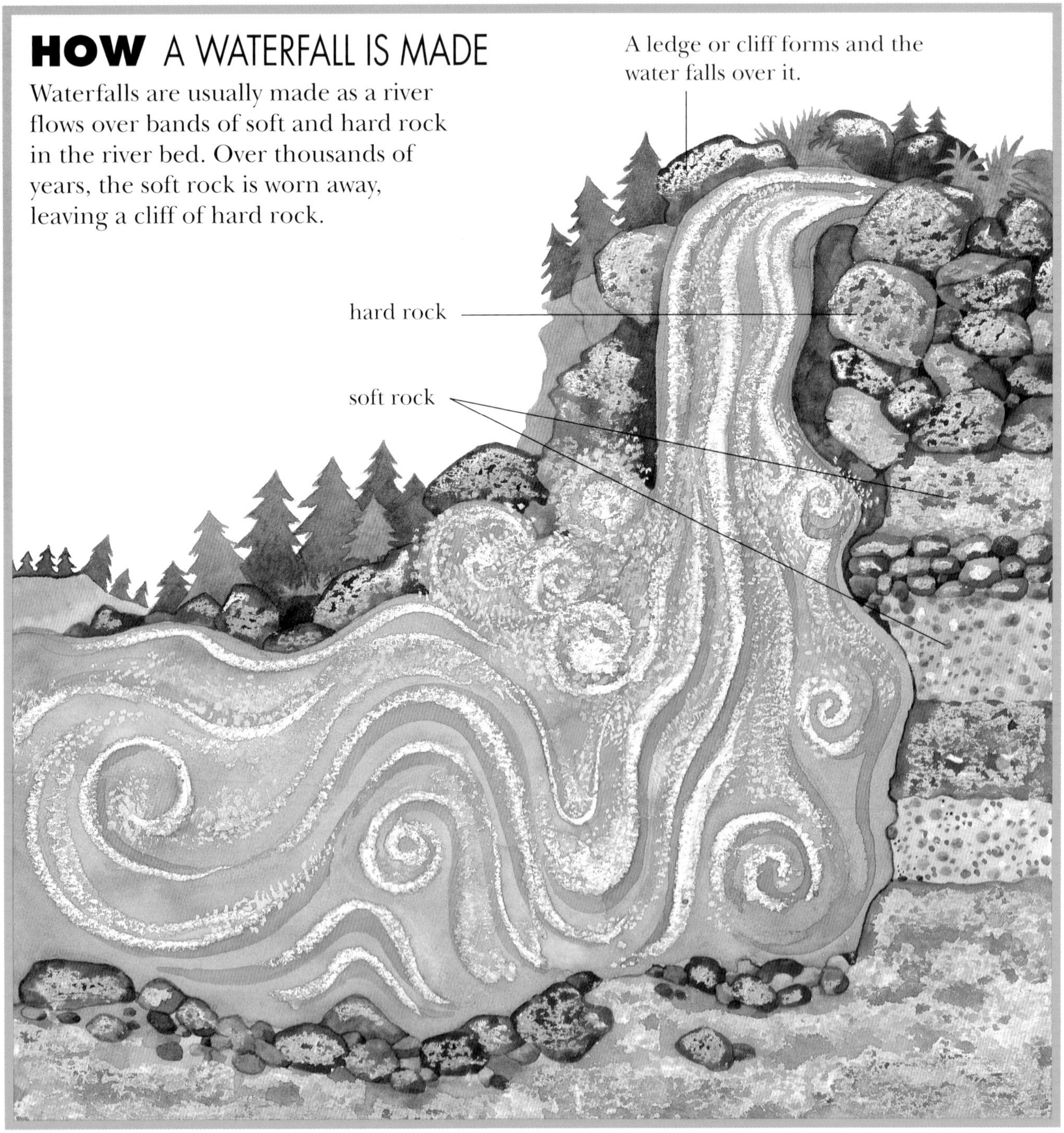
A ledge or cliff forms and the water falls over it.
hard rock
soft rock

FAMOUS WATERFALL

Niagara Falls is one of the world's largest waterfalls. It is on the border of Canada and the USA. It is really two falls, the Horseshoe Falls and the American Falls.

INTERESTING FACT

The highest waterfall in the world is Angel Falls in South America. The water falls 979 metres.

CASCADES AND CATARACTS

- If the amount of water in a waterfall is large, it may be called a cataract. ▶
- If the amount of water in a waterfall is small, it may be called a cascade. Small waterfalls or cascades are often very steep. ▼

WATER SPORTS

SEE ALSO • Canoe • Olympic Games • Sailing • Yacht

Water sports are sports you can play in water.

KINDS OF WATER SPORTS

There are many different kinds of water sports.

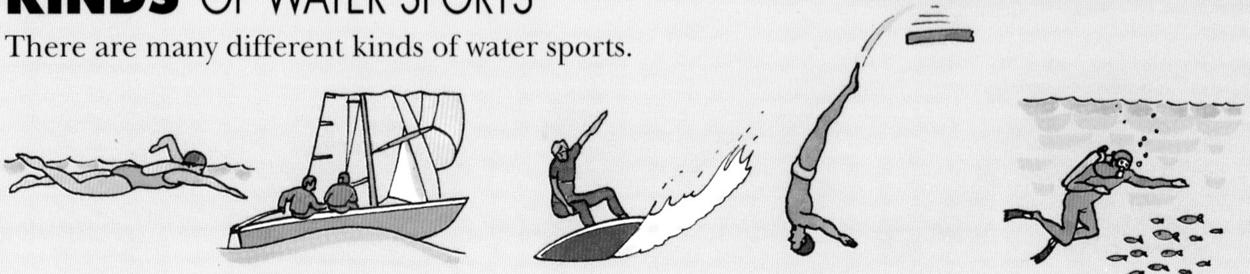

swimming sailing surfing diving scuba diving

snorkelling waterskiing windsurfing canoeing water polo

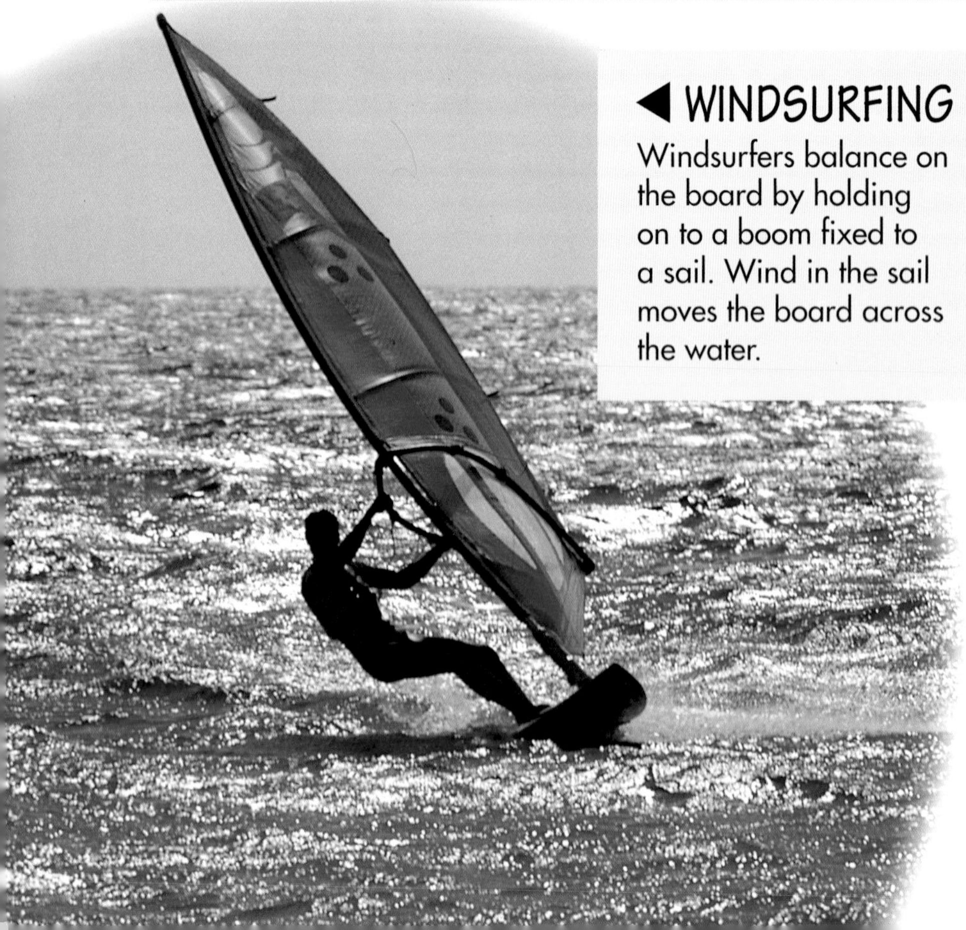

◀ WINDSURFING

Windsurfers balance on the board by holding on to a boom fixed to a sail. Wind in the sail moves the board across the water.

WATERSKIING

People ski on water. They use one or two skis and are towed by a fast powerboat.

WATER POLO

Water polo is played with two teams of seven players. Each team tries to throw the ball into the other team's goal.

SCUBA DIVING ▶

Scuba divers use a face mask, oxygen tanks and breathing apparatus to look at life under the sea.

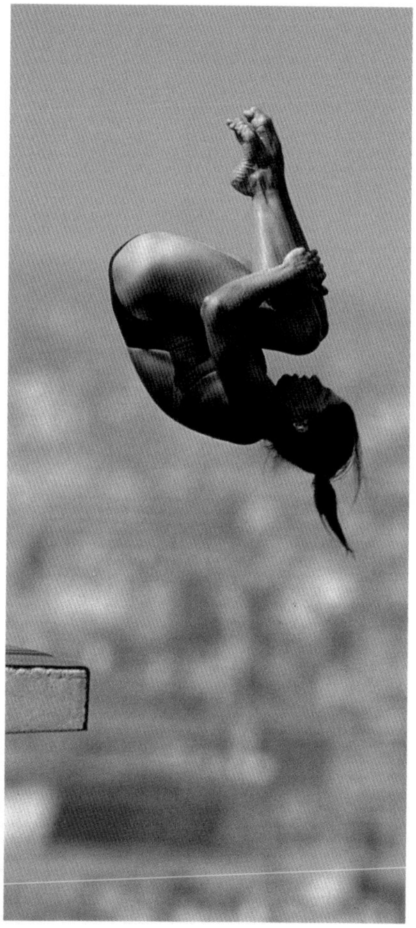

DIVING ▲

Diving is an Olympic sport. Divers dive from platforms ten metres above the water. They can also dive from springboards three metres above the water. Divers win points by the way they dive and by doing difficult dives.

SWIMMING STROKES

Swimmers move through the water using their arms and legs. These actions are called strokes.

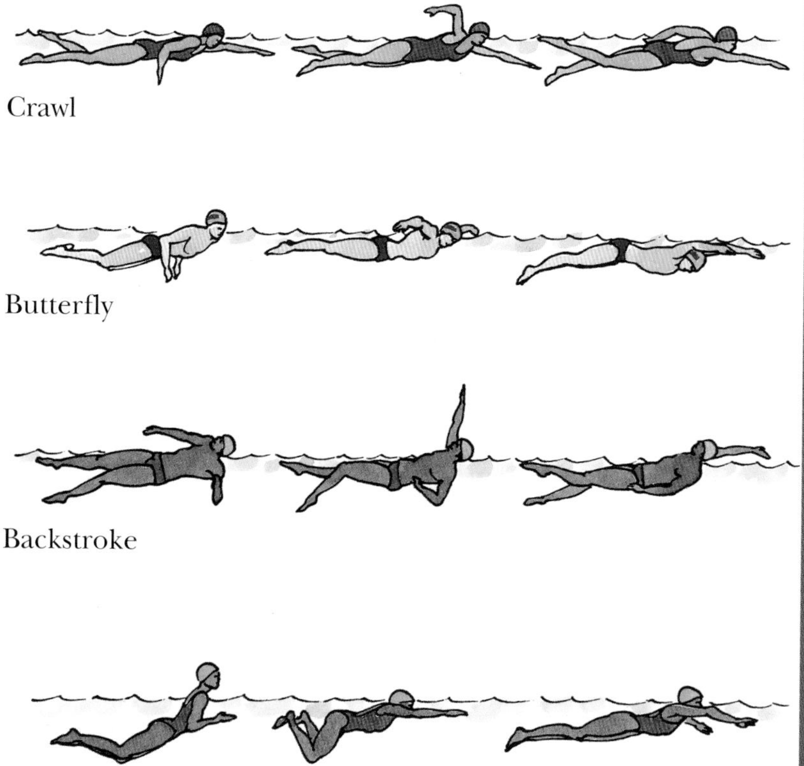

Crawl

Butterfly

Backstroke

Breast stroke

WEASEL

SEE ALSO • Animal • Camouflage • Mammal

A weasel is a small, furry mammal. It has a long, thin body. Weasels are hunting animals. They belong to the same family as stoats.

PARTS OF A WEASEL

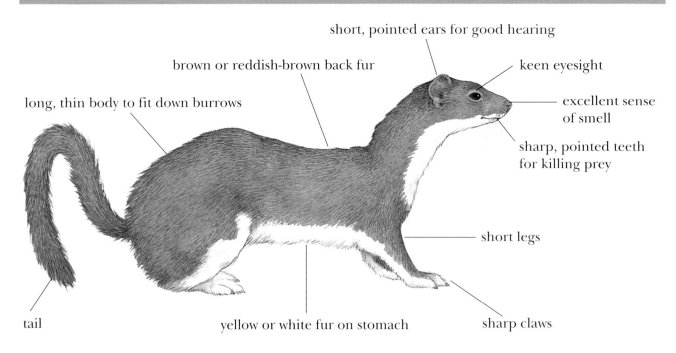

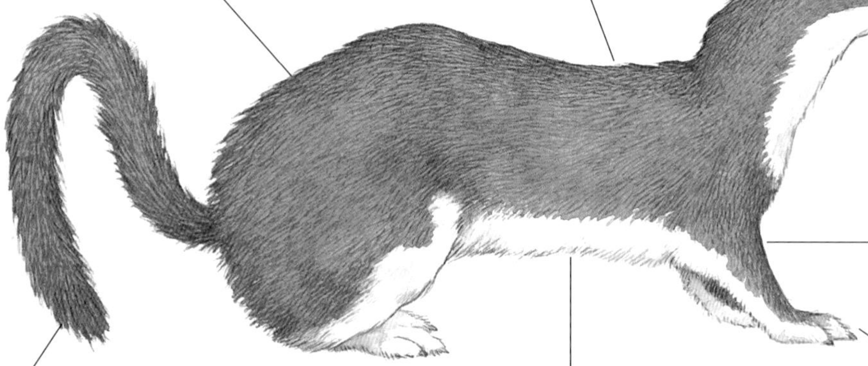

Length: 30 to 45 centimetres including tail
Weight: 400 grams

FOOD

Weasels hunt animals for food. They are carnivores.

HOW WEASELS MOVE

Weasels are hunters. They use their long, thin bodies to reach into burrows to hunt rabbits and other rodents.

WHERE WEASELS LIVE

- ● Europe
- ■ Asia
- ◆ Africa
- ★ North America
- ▲ South America

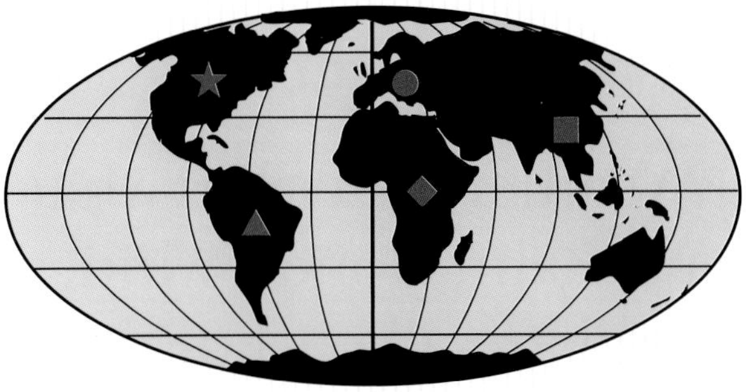

HOW WEASELS LIVE

- Weasels nest in rock piles, tree hollows and unused burrows.
- The female weasel gives birth to between four and eight young at a time.
- After a few weeks, the young weasels leave the burrow to learn to hunt.

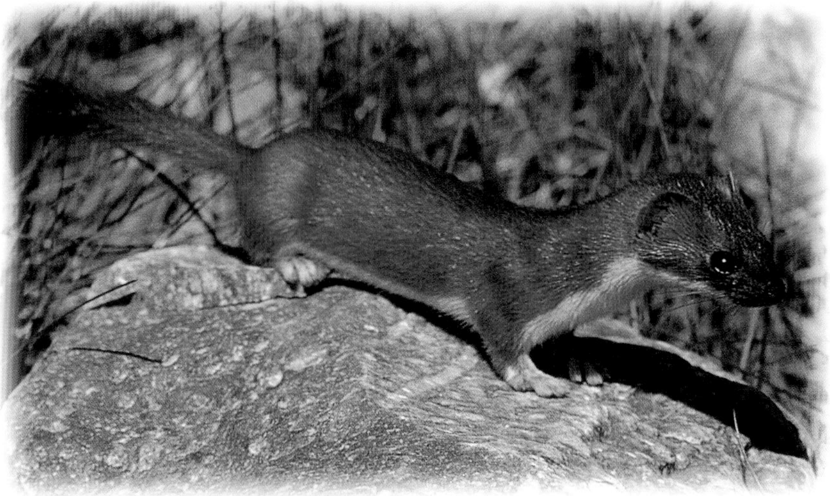

◀ STOATS

Stoats are larger than weasels. They have brown fur with a black tip on their tail. In winter, their fur turns white. This makes them difficult to see in the snow. They are camouflaged.

MEMBERS OF THE WEASEL FAMILY

badger

ferret

otter

skunk

stoat

polecat

marten

WEATHER

SEE ALSO • Cloud • Cyclone • Satellite • Sun • Water • Wind

Weather describes what is happening in the air around us. Rain, clouds, wind, snow, sunshine, and the heat or cold are all part of the weather. Weather changes all the time.

ENERGY FROM THE SUN CAUSES THE WEATHER

- The Sun heats the air around the Earth. Some places get more heat than others.

- The air in some places is warmer than in others. The warm air rises. Cool air is sucked in to replace the warm air. This causes wind.

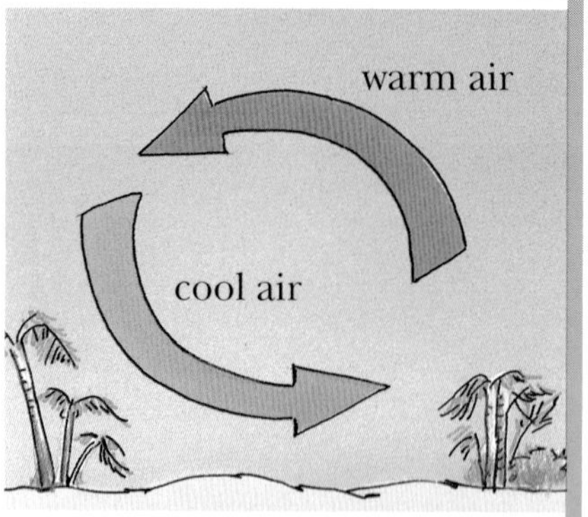

- The Sun heats the water. Some water evaporates into the air as water vapour. When the air cools, the water vapour turns into water droplets which form clouds. Rain falls from the clouds.

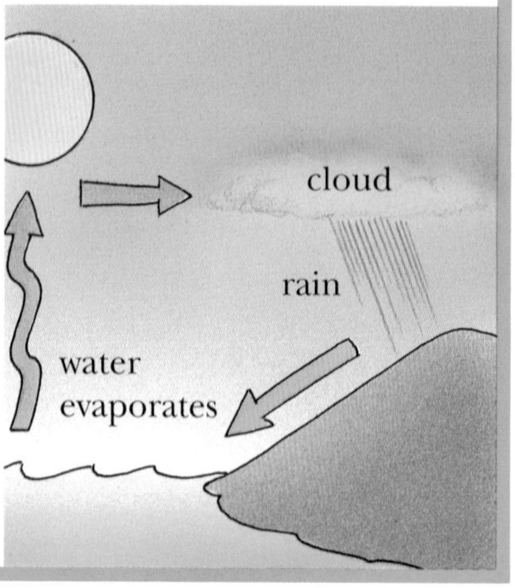

RAIN

The Earth uses the same water over and over again. Without rain, plants would die. People and animals would not have enough food to eat.

INTERESTING FACT

Climate is the pattern of weather in one place.

SNOW

Snow is frozen water droplets in the air. Each droplet forms a crystal. As they fall, the crystals join together to form snowflakes.

INTERESTING FACT

Sleet is a mixture of rain and snow.

DEW

Dew is droplets of water. It forms on clear nights when water vapour in the air changes into water droplets.

FROST

Frost is frozen dew. It forms when the air cools to below zero degrees Celsius. In winter most mornings are frosty in cold countries.

▼

HAIL ▼

Hailstones are small balls of ice. They are made in cold weather. Water droplets freeze at the top of storm clouds. They are made of layers of ice.

INTERESTING FACT

Clouds are made of billions of tiny water droplets.

FOG AND MIST ▶

Fog and mist are low clouds that surround us. Fog is thicker than mist. It is difficult to see in a fog. Fog can stop aeroplanes taking off and landing.

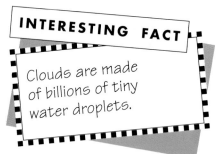

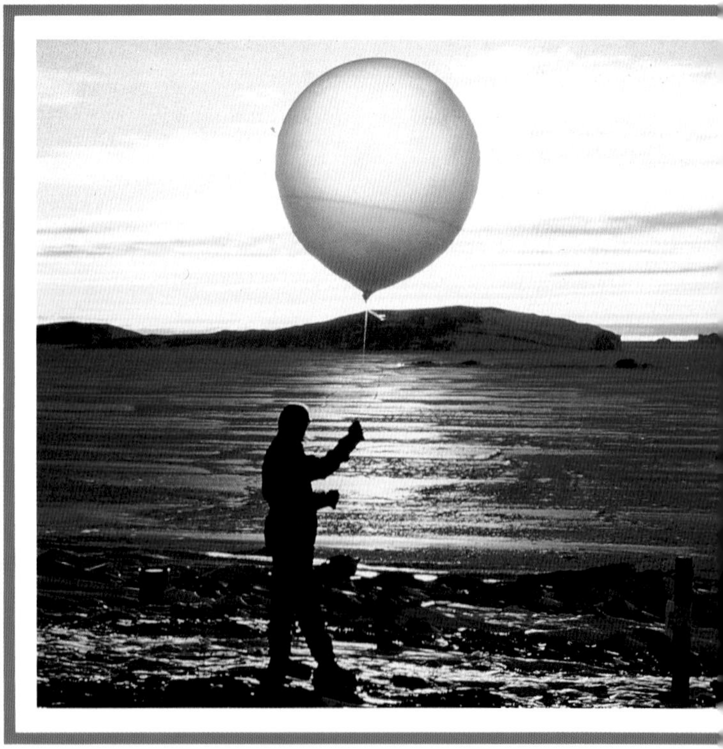

THUNDERSTORMS ▲ AND LIGHTNING

Lightning is an electric spark. It flashes from one cloud to another, or from a cloud to the ground. When the air is heated by a flash of lightning, it expands suddenly. This makes a loud clap of thunder.

AIR PRESSURE

The Earth is surrounded by a layer of air which presses down on the Earth's surface. This is air pressure. Air pressure varies from place to place.

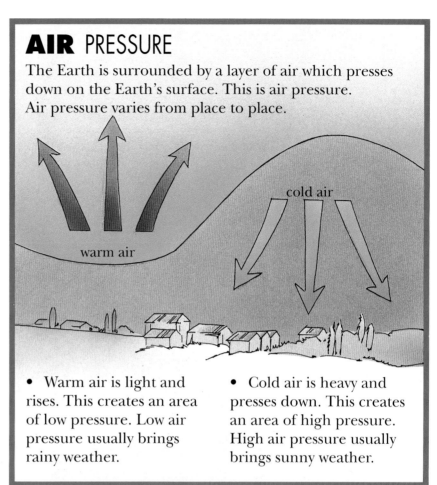

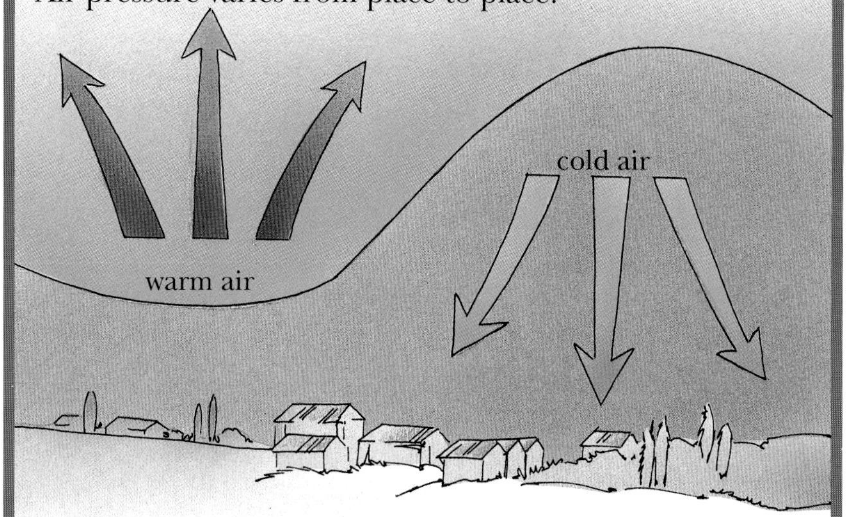

- Warm air is light and rises. This creates an area of low pressure. Low air pressure usually brings rainy weather.
- Cold air is heavy and presses down. This creates an area of high pressure. High air pressure usually brings sunny weather.

FORECASTING THE WEATHER

Weather forecasters tell us what the weather will be like tomorrow. They warn us about dangerous weather such as storms.

- Weather forecasters collect information about the weather. They use weather balloons, radar and satellites to watch the weather. They use special instruments to measure wind, rain and air pressure.
- They use computers to study the information.
- The computers turn the information into weather maps.

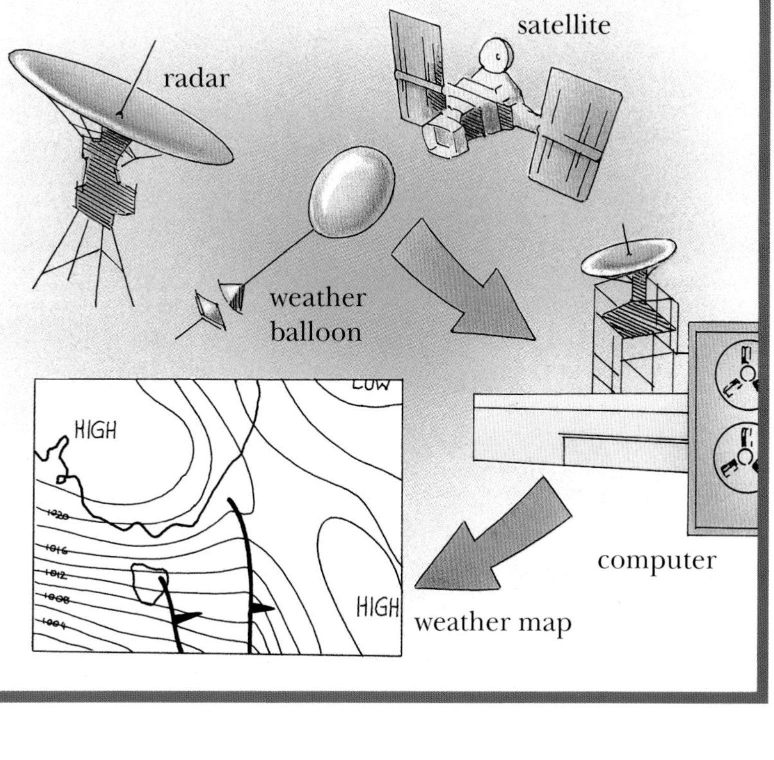

WHALE

SEE ALSO • Animal • Dolphin • Mammal

A whale is a large sea mammal. Whales spend most of their time under water. They come to the surface to breathe. Whales are the largest animals.

PARTS OF A BLUE WHALE

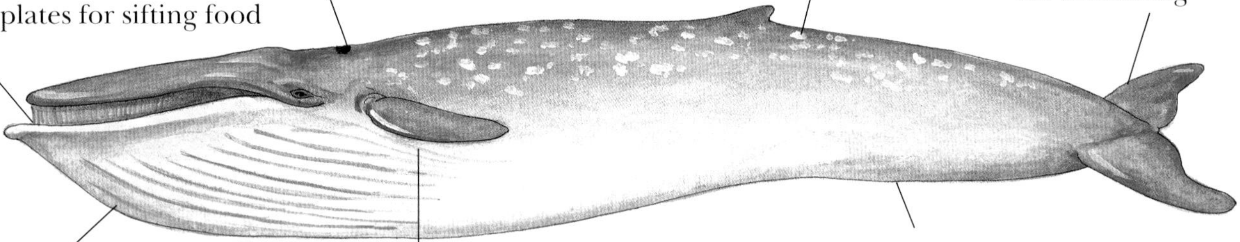

Whales have a thick layer of blubber (fat) under their skin which keeps out the cold.

Weight: more than 200 tonnes **Length**: 30 metres

KINDS OF WHALES

There are two main kinds of whales – toothed whales and baleen whales.

Baleen whales are whales without teeth. They have comb-like baleen plates on their jaws which filter the krill they eat.

Toothed whales have dozens of sharp teeth for gripping prey.

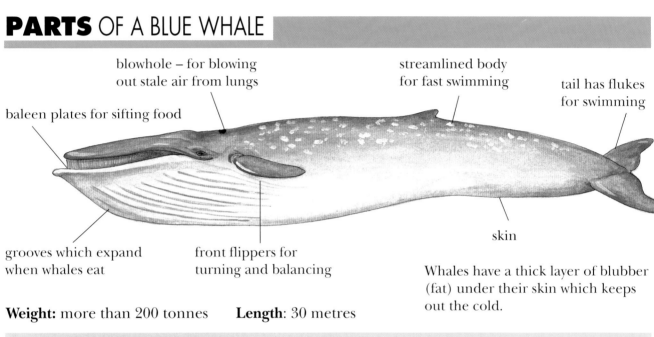

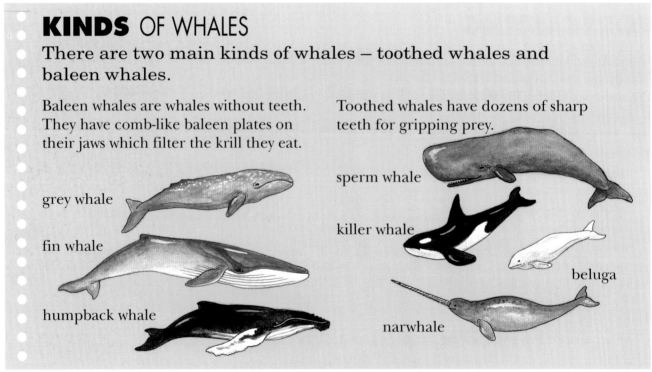

FOOD

Toothed whales

INTERESTING FACT

A female whale is called a cow. A male whale is called a bull. A young whale is called a calf.

HOW WHALES MOVE

- A whale swims by beating its tail up and down.
- Whales can dive to great depths and can stay there for about 45 minutes at a time. They sleep by napping for a few minutes at a time.

WHALE SOUNDS

Whales have excellent hearing. They make sounds to call to other whales. The sounds they make travel for great distances underwater.

HOW WHALES LIVE

- Some whales live in groups called pods, schools or herds.
- A female whale usually gives birth to one calf at a time.
- As soon as the calf is born, it swims up to the surface of the water to breathe. The female whale feeds her calf with her milk underwater.

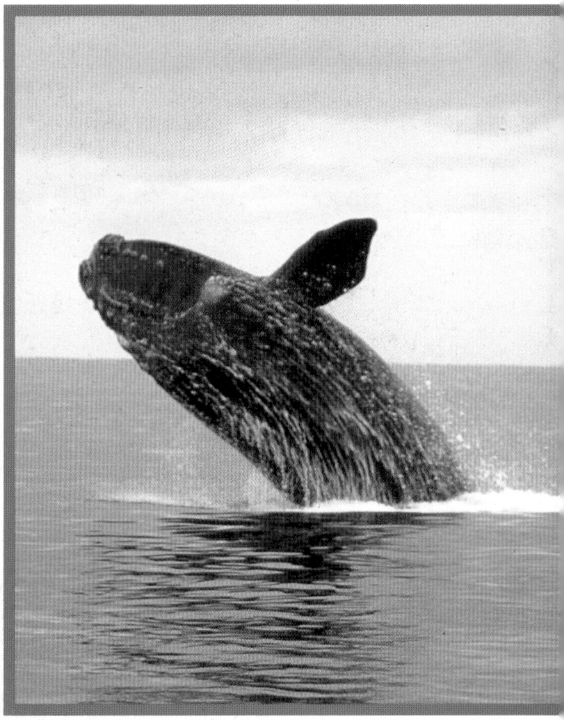

ENDANGERED SPECIES

Some whales have become scarce. For hundreds of years, people have hunted whales for oil. Today, many countries have joined together to protect whales.

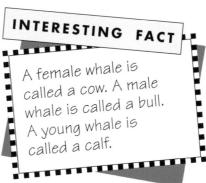

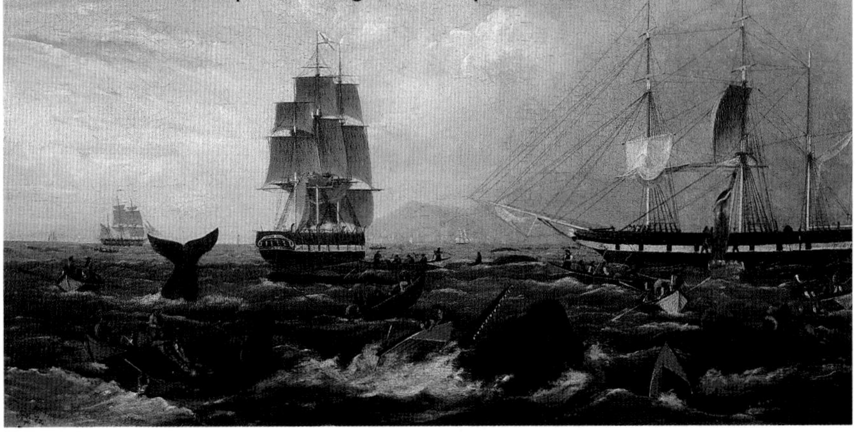

WHERE WHALES LIVE

Whales live in oceans all over the world. Some whales live in rivers.

WHEEL

SEE ALSO • Bicycle • Invention • Machine • Motor Car

A wheel is round. It moves by rolling or spinning. Wheels are used to move things. They are also used to control the flow of power.

HISTORY

• Before wheels were invented, people pushed or dragged heavy loads.

• The wheel was invented about 5000 years ago. Animals were used to move loads.

• Wheels with spokes were first used about 4000 years ago. Carriage wheels have spokes.

INSIDE A CAR

Many different kinds of wheels are used inside a car. Wheels are used in all kinds of transport.

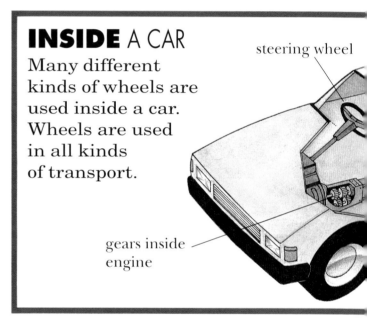

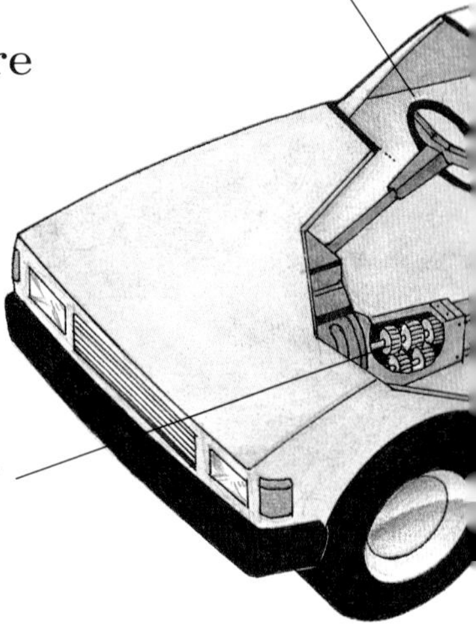

INTERESTING FACT

Most machines and engines use wheels.

WHEEL AND AXLE

The wheel and axle is a simple machine. When the wheel is turned, the axle also turns and lifts the weight.

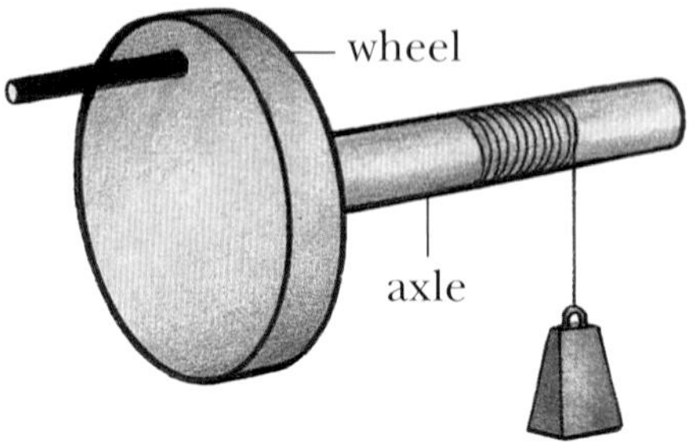

PULLEY ▶

A pulley makes lifting easier.

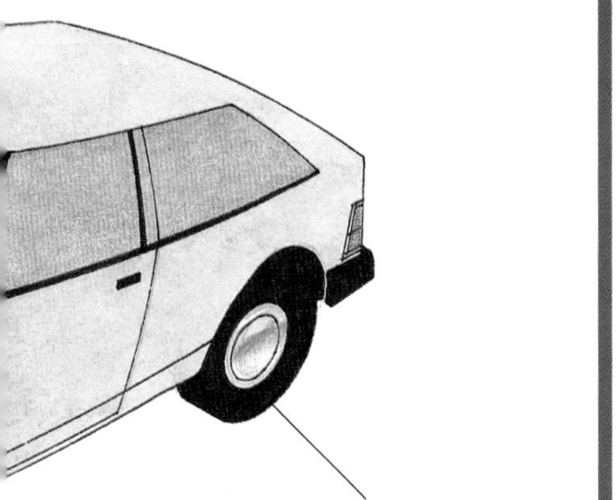

hollow rubber tyres filled with air

BALL BEARINGS

Ball bearings are small steel balls. Ball bearings are used inside bicycle wheels. They keep wheels turning easily on their axles.

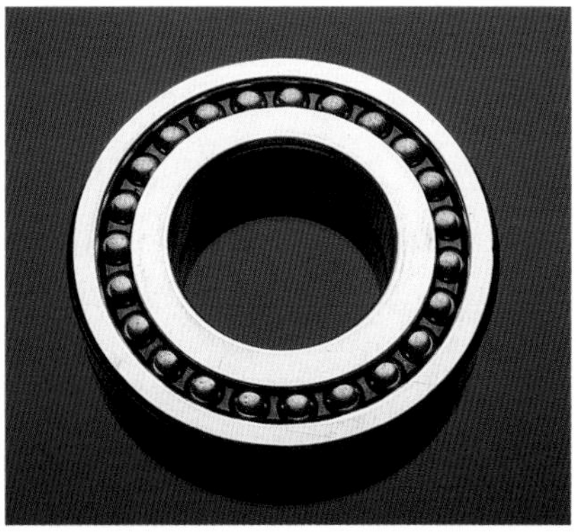

GEARS

Gears are notched edges on wheels. They help to work all kinds of machines.

Gears connect with one another. They transfer power from one gear to another. They can be used to speed up or slow down a machine.

◀ WATERWHEELS

Waterwheels are used to drive simple machines. They spin as water flows under or over them. The wheel drives machinery. Waterwheels turn millstones which grind wheat into flour.

WIND

SEE ALSO • Air • Atmosphere • Cyclone • Weather

Wind is moving air. You cannot see wind, but you can feel it. You can see it move branches and other things. Winds can be as gentle as a light breeze and as strong as a hurricane.

WHERE WINDS BLOW

Winds blow in the troposphere. The troposphere is the lowest layer of the atmosphere.

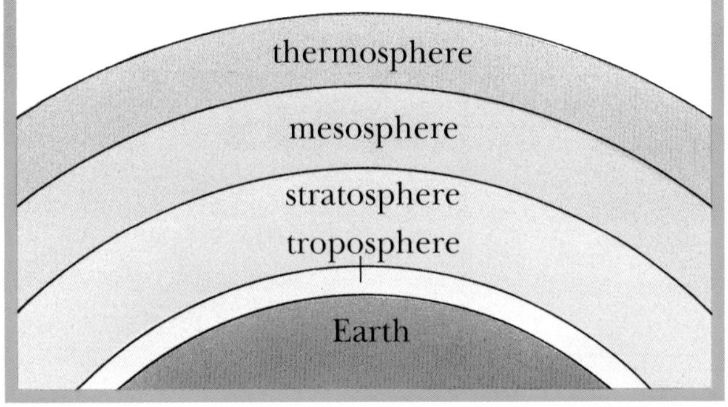

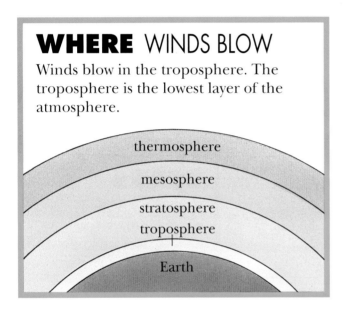

HOW WIND IS MADE

Wind is caused by the Sun heating the air around the Earth unevenly.

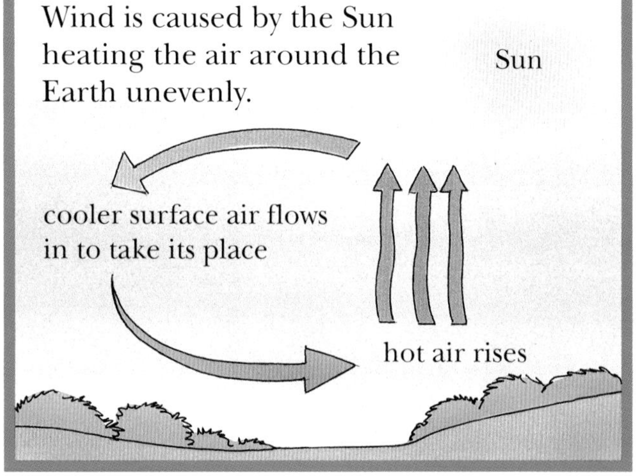

HOW A SEA BREEZE IS MADE

During the day, the Sun heats up the land faster than it heats the sea. Warm air rises over the land. Cooler air from the sea flows in to replace it. A cool sea breeze is made.

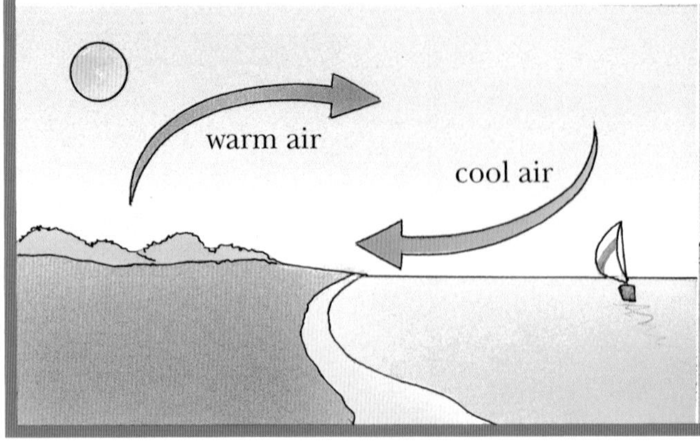

HOW A LAND BREEZE IS MADE

At night, the sea holds its heat longer than the land. Warm air rises over the sea. Cool air from the land flows in to replace it. A cool land breeze is made.

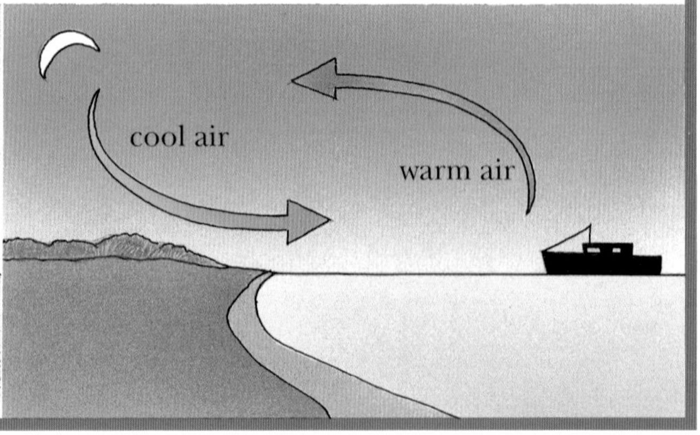

WIND IS PART OF THE WEATHER

- A hot day can turn cool if a wind blows from a cool area.
- A cool day can become hot if a wind blows the clouds away and lets the Sun shine.

INTERESTING FACT

Winds are named after the direction they blow from. A north wind blows from north to south.

MEASURING THE WIND

- The speed of wind is measured by an instrument called an anemometer. ▶
- The direction of the wind is measured with a weathervane. ▼

- Balloons filled with helium are used to measure the wind above the Earth's surface. ▶

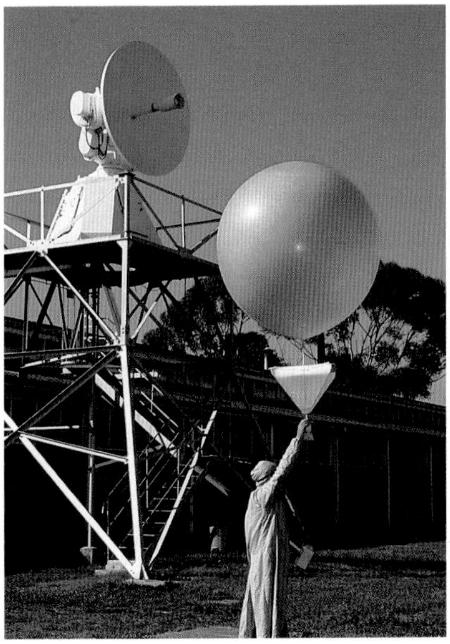

THE BEAUFORT WIND SCALE

The Beaufort Wind Scale is used to measure the strength of wind. It goes from Force 0 to Force 12.

Force 0 – Calm
Smoke rises straight up.

Force 3 – Gentle breeze
Leaves and small twigs on trees move.

Force 9 – Strong gale
Branches break off trees.

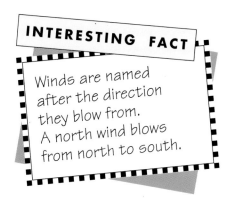

Force 12 – Hurricane
Buildings are damaged.

WOLF

SEE ALSO • Animal • Dog • Endangered Species • Mammal

A wolf is a wild mammal. It is the largest member of the dog family. It looks like a dog, but it is bigger and stronger. Wolves hunt for food.

PARTS OF A GREY WOLF

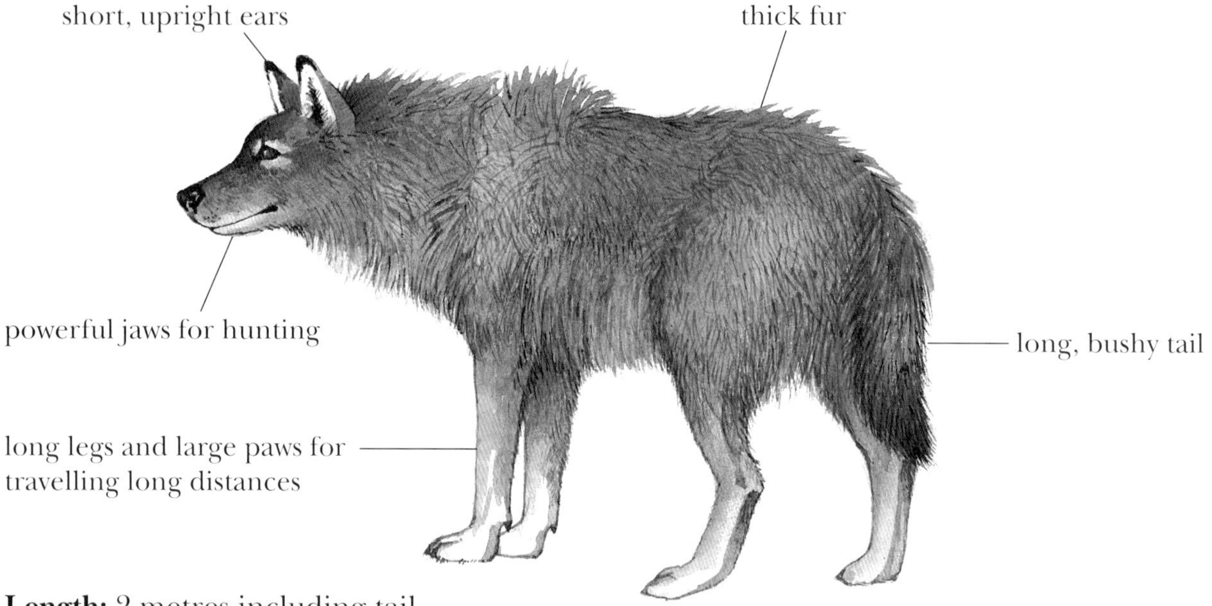

Length: 2 metres including tail
Weight: 50 kilograms

HOW WOLVES LIVE

- Most wolves live in family groups called packs. A pack stays together for a long time. Wolves often stay with the same mate all their lives.
- A female wolf gives birth to 1 to 11 pups in the spring. They are born in a den dug in the earth.
- The pups feed on their mother's milk.
- Both parents train the pups to hunt.

WHERE WOLVES LIVE

- ● North America
- ■ Greenland
- ◆ Europe
- ▲ Asia
- ★ Canada
- ▼ Alaska

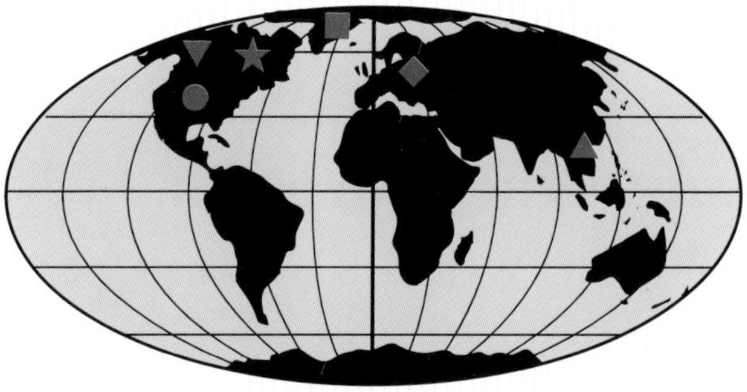

FOOD

Wolves eat other animals. They are carnivores.

smaller animals

rodents

birds

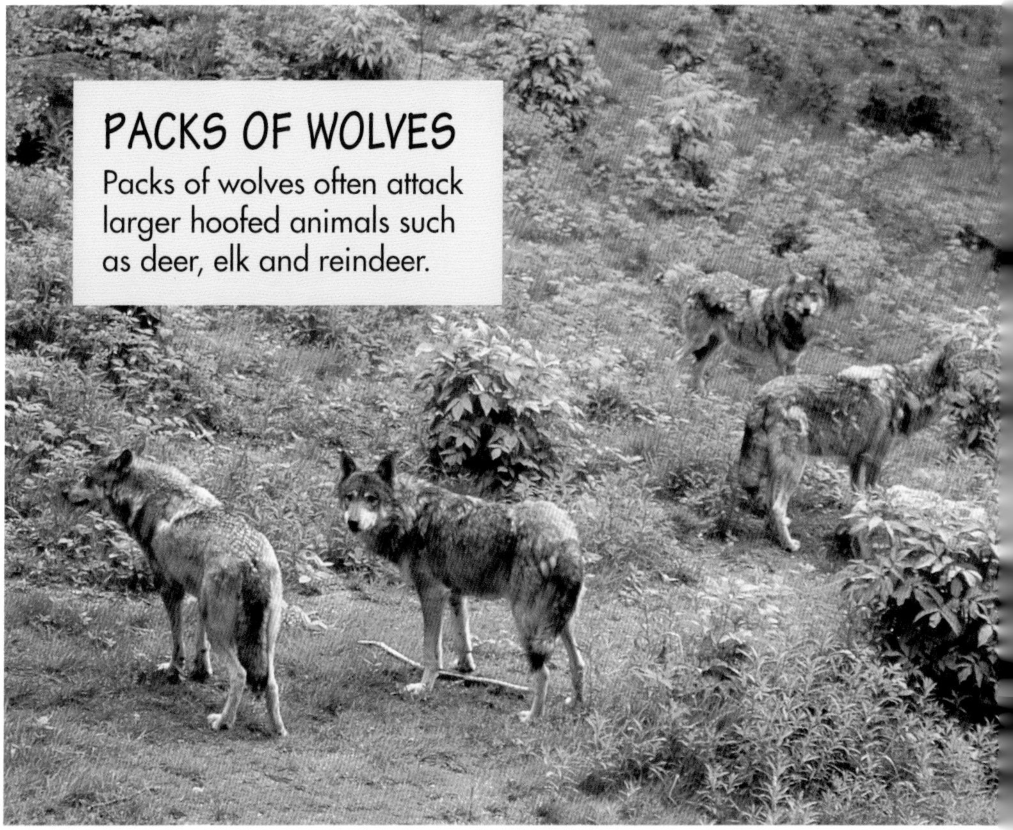

PACKS OF WOLVES

Packs of wolves often attack larger hoofed animals such as deer, elk and reindeer.

ENDANGERED SPECIES

For many years, people have hunted wolves for their fur. People have also killed wolves because they hunt farm animals. Today, many wolves are endangered. The maned wolf is an endangered wolf.

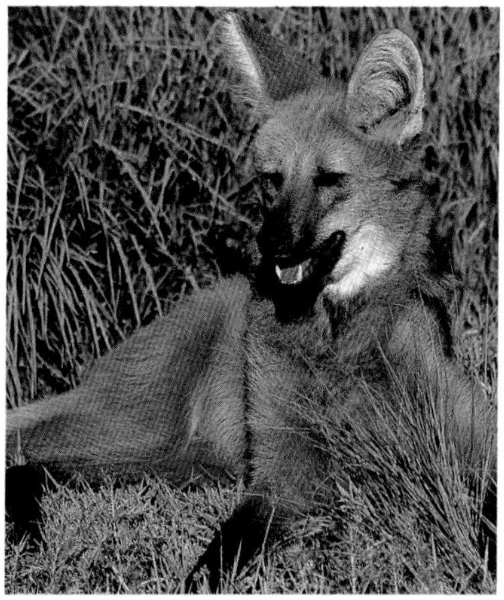

WORM

SEE ALSO • Animal • Earthworm • Compost • Invertebrate

A worm is an animal which has a soft body and no legs. Some worms are very small and others are very long. There are many different kinds of worms.

KINDS OF WORMS

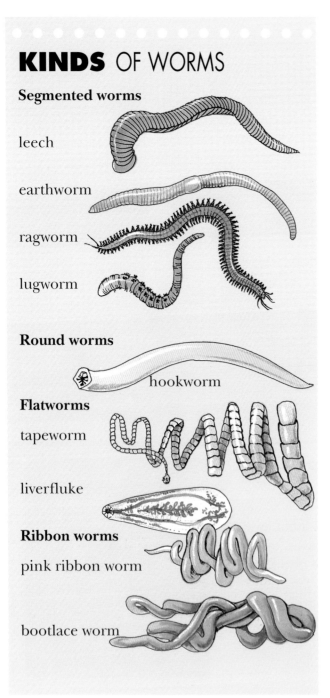

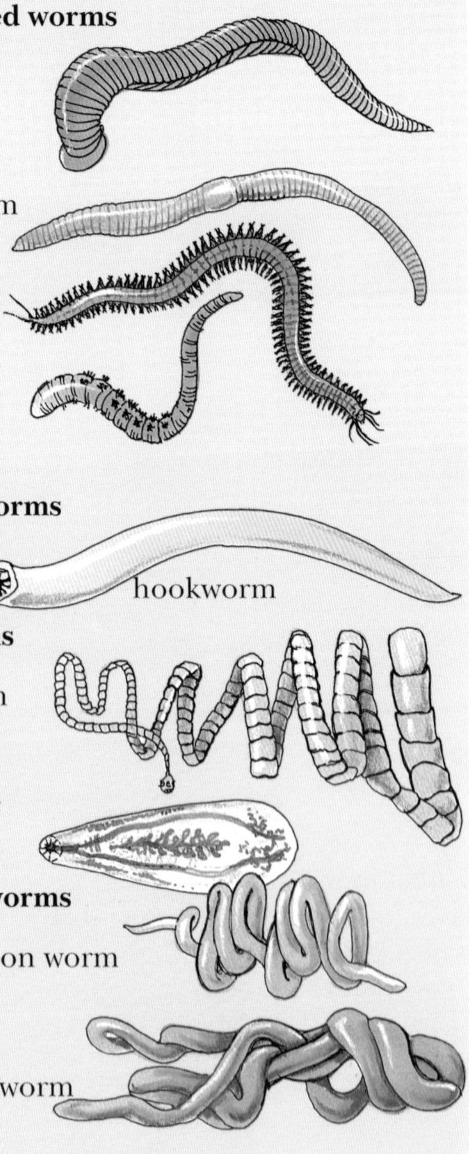

WHERE WORMS LIVE

Some worms live in soil, some live in water and some live in rotting plant and animal material. Some worms are parasites and live inside animals or plants.

SEASHORE WORMS

Lugworms live in U-shaped burrows. They eat sand and mud.

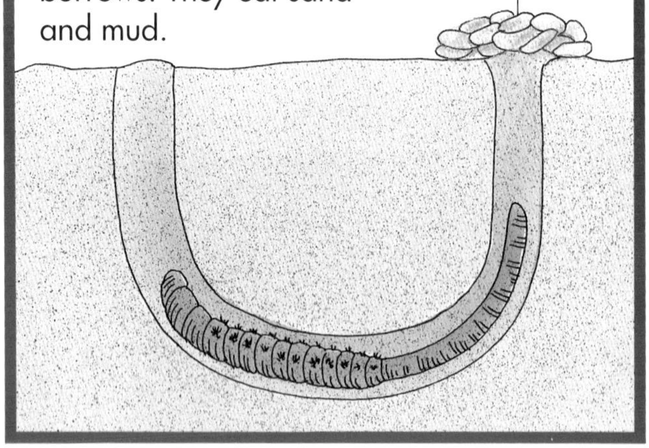

EARTHWORMS

Earthworms live in soil. They dig burrows, letting in water and air. Earthworms eat soil as they burrow. The undigested soil comes out as worm casts.

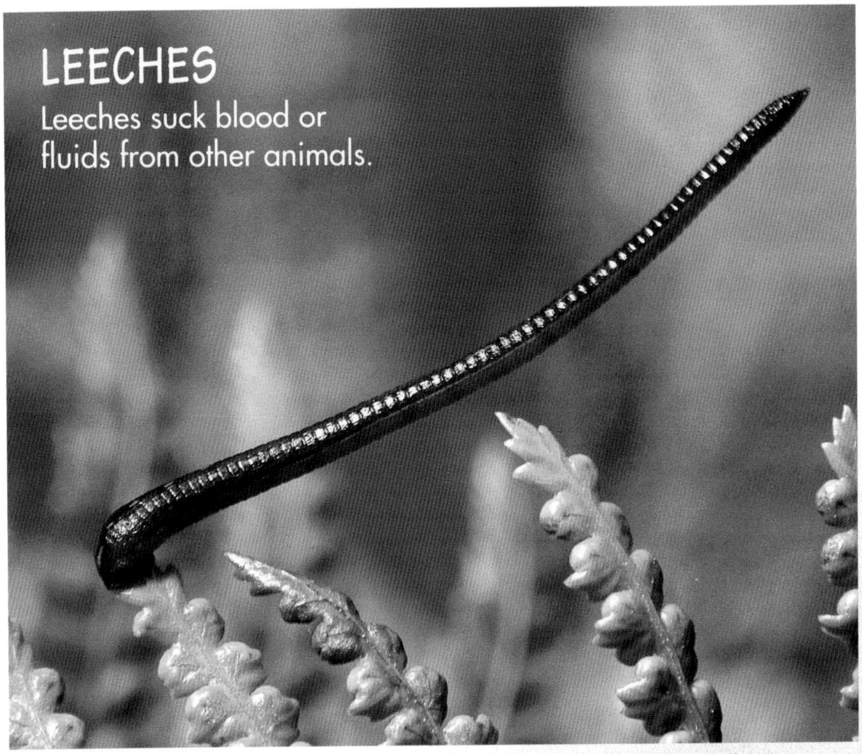

LEECHES

Leeches suck blood or fluids from other animals.

INTERESTING FACT

An earthworm has five pairs of hearts. They help circulate the worm's blood.

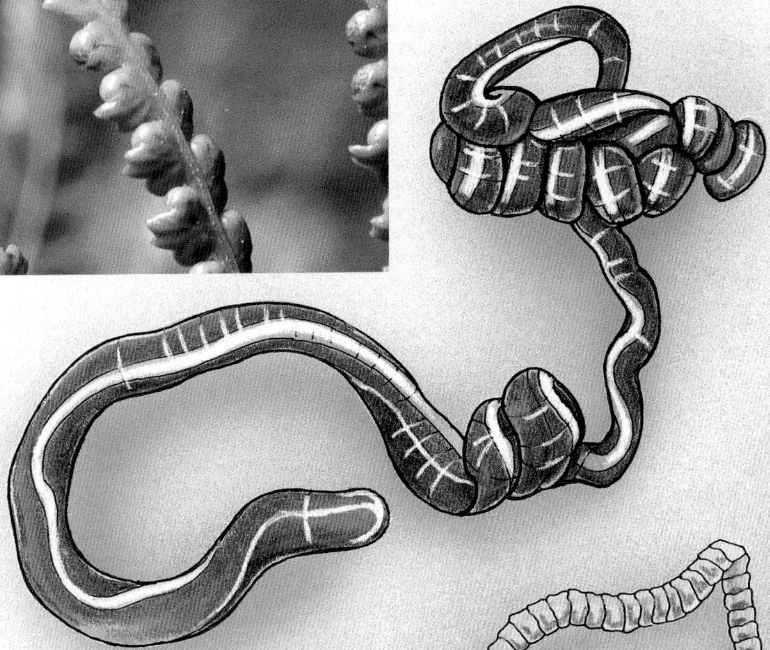

RIBBON WORMS ▶

Ribbon worms feed on other animals such as worms and shellfish. Some are brightly coloured, while others are dull. Some are only a few centimetres long, and others are up to one metre long.

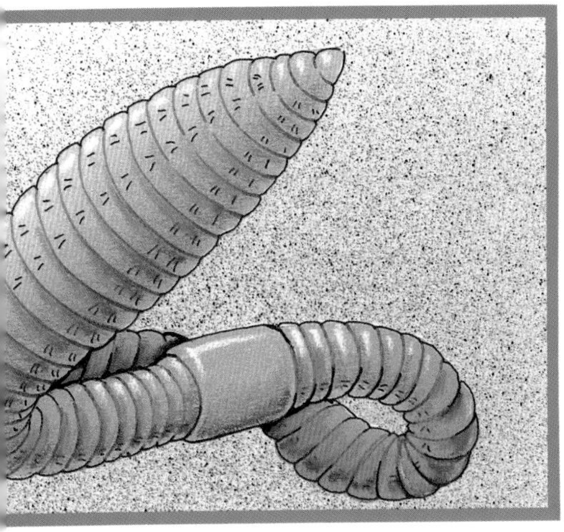

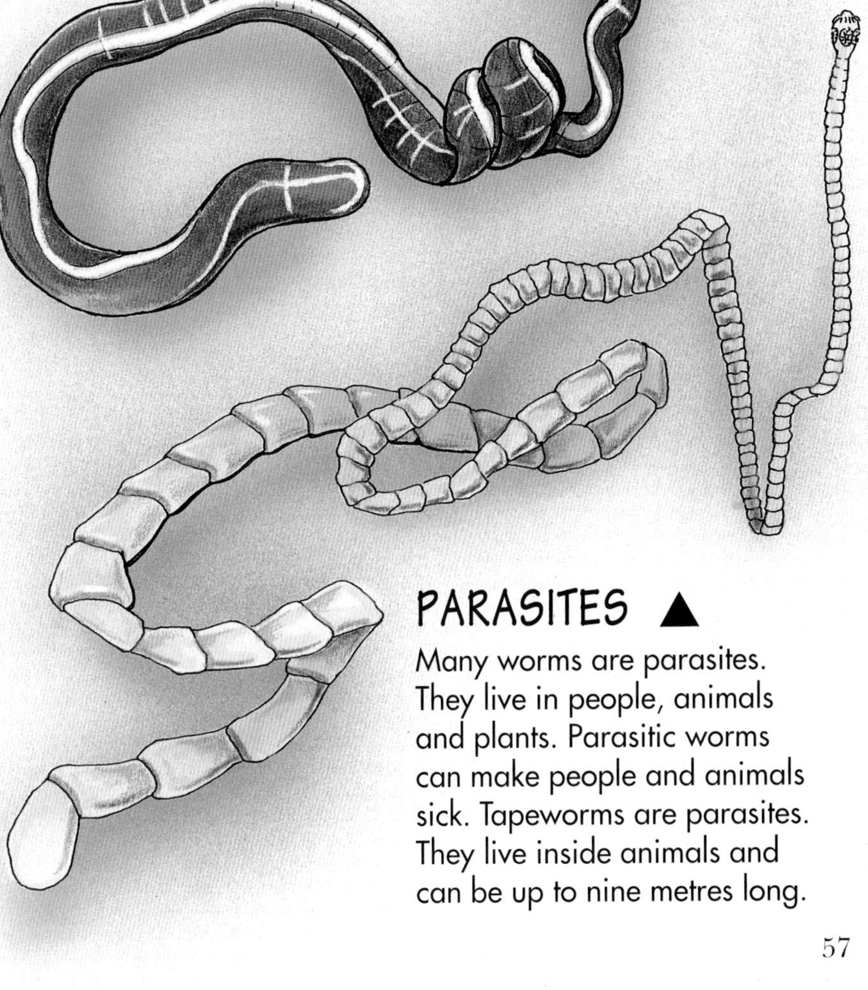

PARASITES ▲

Many worms are parasites. They live in people, animals and plants. Parasitic worms can make people and animals sick. Tapeworms are parasites. They live inside animals and can be up to nine metres long.

X-RAYS

SEE ALSO • Airport • Doctor • Hospital • Radio • Skeleton

X-rays are invisible rays of energy. They can pass through soft materials such as flesh and skin. X-rays cannot pass through hard materials such as metal and bone. X-rays are used to take a photograph of the inside of your body.

HOW X-RAYS WORK

X-rays leave an image of what they have passed through on a photographic plate.

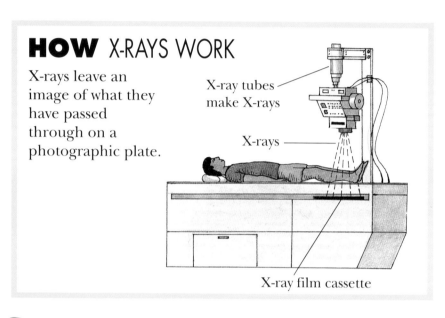

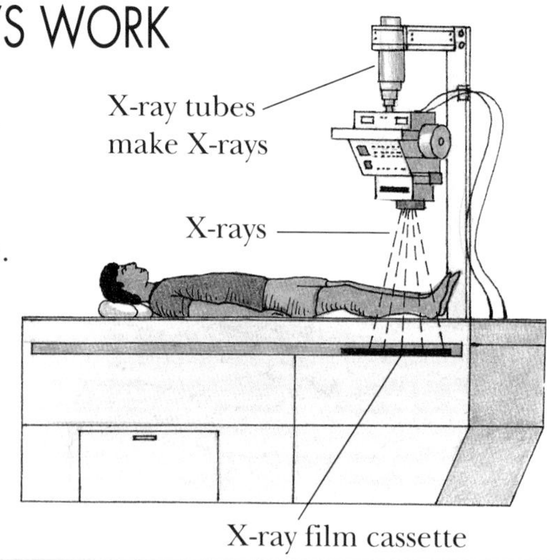

HISTORY ▼

X-rays were discovered in 1895 by Wilhelm Roentgen, a German scientist. He named them X-rays because he did not know what they were.

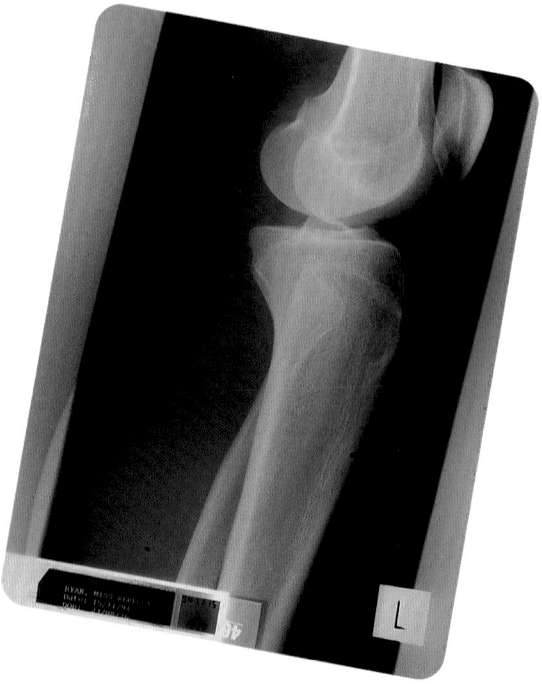

◀ MEDICAL X-RAYS

Doctors and dentists use an X-ray camera to take photographs of bones, body organs and teeth. When the film is developed, the bone shows up as a shadow because X-rays cannot pass through bone.

INTERESTING FACT

The Sun, stars and other objects in space produce X-rays naturally.

LUGGAGE SCANNER

Airports use X-rays to find dangerous metal weapons and objects in luggage. Metal objects show up as a shadow on the X-ray photograph.

XYLOPHONE

SEE ALSO • Music • Orchestra

A xylophone is a musical instrument. It has rows of wooden or metal bars fixed to a frame. The bars are struck to make a clear sound like a bell.

PARTS OF A XYLOPHONE

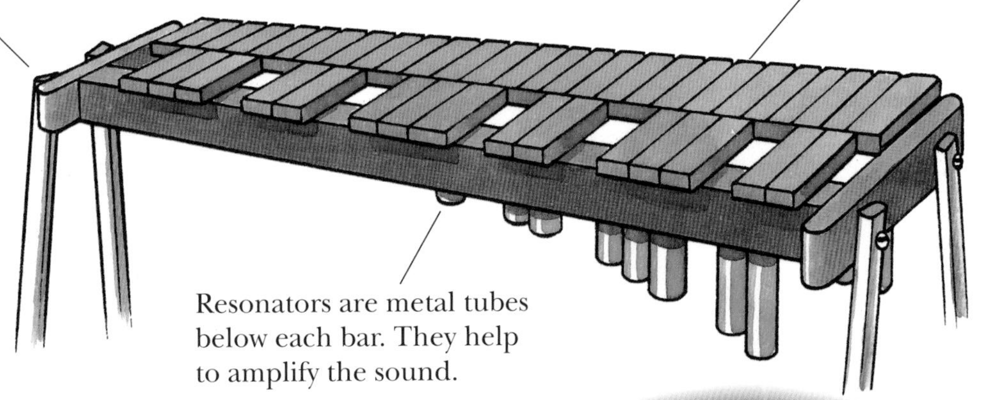

PLAYING THE XYLOPHONE ▶

A xylophone player strikes the sounding bars with hard mallets. Xylophones are used in orchestras and bands. They belong to the percussion section of the orchestra. They can also be used to play solo pieces of music.

INTERESTING FACT

A vibraphone is an electric xylophone.

YACHT

SEE ALSO • Boat • Floating • Sailing • Ship • Transport

A yacht is a sailing boat. It is moved by wind in its sails. Small yachts can be sailed by one person. Large ocean-going yachts can have a crew of 20 or more.

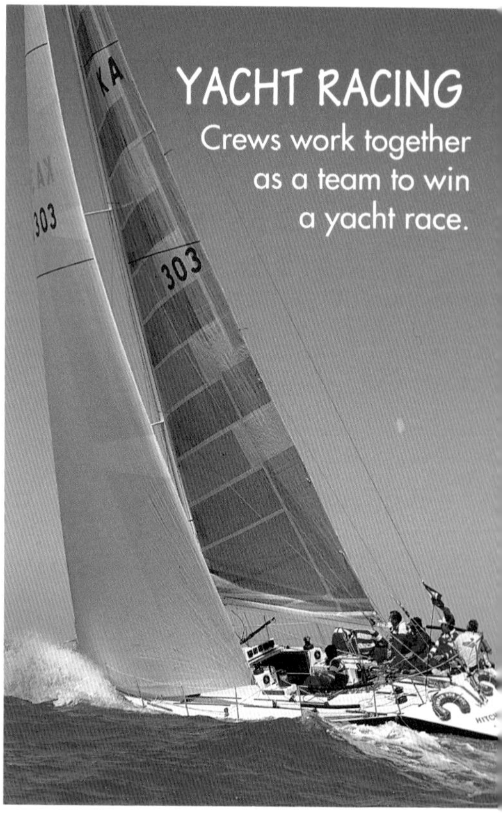

PARTS OF A YACHT

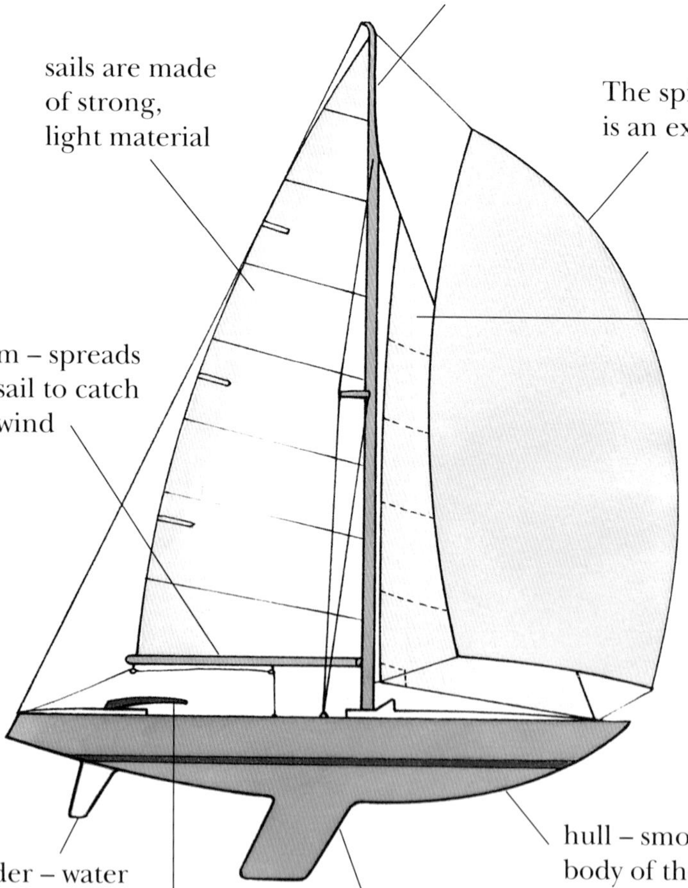

SITTING OUT ▼

Sitting out is putting your weight outside of the yacht to keep it upright.

YAK

SEE ALSO • Animal • Cattle • Mammal • Ungulates

A yak is a large mammal with long, shaggy fur. It belongs to the cattle family. Most yaks live in the wild on the mountains of Tibet and China.

PARTS OF A YAK

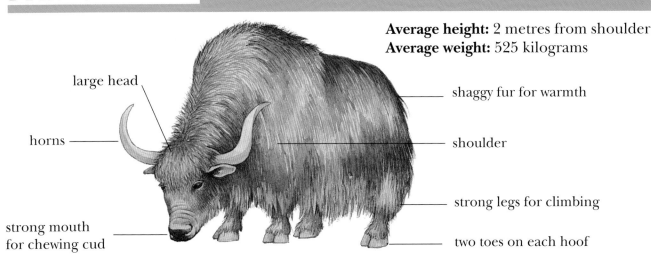

Average height: 2 metres from shoulder
Average weight: 525 kilograms

FOOD

Yaks eat plants.
They are herbivores.

PACK ANIMALS

Yaks are used as pack animals. A yak can carry a heavy load for up to 30 kilometres a day.

HOW YAKS LIVE

Yaks usually have one calf at a time. They are good climbers even when they are young.

ZEBRA

SEE ALSO • Animal • Grassland • Horse • Mammal • Ungulates

A zebra is a wild horse. It has a black and white striped body. Some zebras live on open grassy plains. Some live in the mountains.

PARTS OF A COMMON ZEBRA

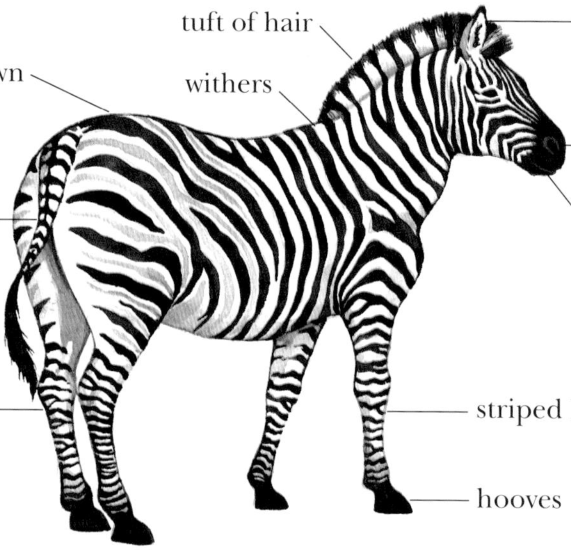

Height: 120 to 150 centimetres from withers

WHERE ZEBRAS LIVE

● Africa

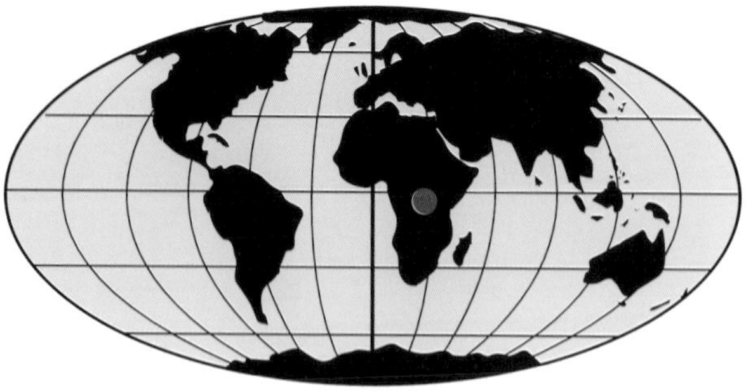

HOW ZEBRAS LIVE

- Zebras live in herds. The herd is led by a male zebra (stallion).
- The female zebra (mare) gives birth to one young every spring.
- Zebras often roam the plains with herds of antelopes.

FOOD

Zebras are grazing animals. They eat grass.

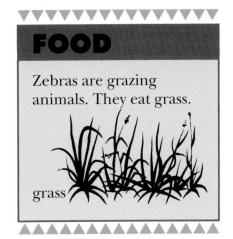

INTERESTING FACT

Every zebra has a different pattern of stripes.

HOW ZEBRAS MOVE

Zebras can run quickly to escape from enemies such as cheetahs. They can run at a speed of 65 kilometres per hour.

KINDS OF ZEBRAS

There are three kinds of zebras.

- Mountain zebras live in the mountains of Africa. They are the smallest kind of zebra and are rare. ▶

- Grevy's zebra is the biggest zebra. It has more stripes than the common zebra. ▼

- Common zebras live on the grassy plains of Africa. ◀

ZOO

SEE ALSO • Conservation • Endangered Species • Veterinarian

A zoo is a place where wild animals are kept. At zoos, people can see and learn about animals they would not be able to see anywhere else. Zoos help to save rare and endangered animals.

ZOO STAFF

Many people are needed to keep a zoo running well:

- cleaners clean the cages and feed the animals
- cooks
- vets
- nurses
- gardeners
- guides
- builders.

INTERESTING FACT

Zoo is the short word for zoological gardens. A zoologist is a scientist who studies animals.

CONSERVATION

Zoos help to save rare animals from dying out. Zoologists can study animals closely at zoos.

AT THE ZOO

Zoo animals are kept in enclosures. Each enclosure is like the animal's home in the wild.

People can see animals easily at the zoo. The animals are separated from the people by moats, trenches and glass walls.

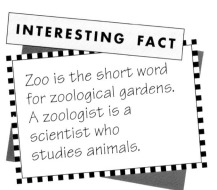